CU
SHOCK!

WORKING HOLIDAYS ABROAD

Work, Earn & Travel Around the World

MARK HEMPSHELL

·K·U·P·E·R·A·R·D·

In the same series

Australia	*Greece*	*Mexico*	*Switzerland*
Bolivia	*Hong Kong*	*Morocco*	*Syria*
Britain	*India*	*Myanmar*	*Taiwan*
California	*Indonesia*	*Nepal*	*Thailand*
Canada	*Iran*	*Netherlands*	*Turkey*
Chile	*Ireland*	*Norway*	*UAE*
China	*Israel*	*Pakistan*	*Ukraine*
Cuba	*Italy*	*Philippines*	*USA*
Czech Republic	*Japan*	*Singapore*	*USA—The South*
Denmark	*Korea*	*South Africa*	*Venezuela*
Egypt	*Laos*	*Spain*	*Vietnam*
France	*Malaysia*	*Sri Lanka*	
Germany	*Mauritius*	*Sweden*	

A Student's Guide
A Traveller's Medical Guide
Living & Working in Chicago
Living & Working in London
Living & Working in New York
Living & Working in Paris
Living & Working in Rome

Living and Working Abroad—
  A Practical Guide
Living and Working Abroad—
  A Parent's Guide
Living and Working Abroad—
  A Wife's Guide

Culture Shock! Working Holidays Abroad
First published in Great Britain 1996 by
Kuperard
311 Ballards Lane
Finchley
London N12 8LY
Tel: 0181 446 2440 Fax: 0181 446 2441
Email: kuperard@bravo.clara.net

Revised 1999

Kuperard is an imprint of Bravo Ltd.

Illustrations by TRIGG

Printed in Singapore

ISBN 1-85733-266-0

The information provided in this book has been checked at the date of preparation. However, readers are cautioned that particulars, especially pertaining to local laws and addresses, are liable to be changed without notice, and they should therefore check the details for themselves before travelling.

CONTENTS

CHAPTER THREE
PLANNING A SAFE AND ENJOYABLE TRIP

CHAPTER FOUR
OPPORTUNITIES FOR CUT-PRICE TRAVEL

CHAPTER FIVE
COUNTRY-BY-COUNTRY DIRECTORY

CHAPTER SIX
WHERE TO FIND THAT EMBASSY

FOREWORD

Have you ever thought it would be a good idea to travel the world for a while, working as you go? Well, now you can!

It is one thing to think about doing it, of course, but another to travel around and find work in a foreign country, especially when the local culture is so different from the one you are used to. That is why we have put together this book of helpful information. It is also a directory of contacts covering every corner of the world—allowing you to find out about opportunities and vacancies before you even leave home.

This book is jam-packed with ideas and newly updated contacts for your working holiday. These job opportunities will not make you a millionaire, but will pay for your food and accommodation (some of them offer free food and accommodation). It will also fund your onward journey to your next exciting port of call, wherever that might be.

In this book, you will find opportunities in the hotel and restaurant trade, tourism, construction, agriculture and farming, au pairing and nannying, voluntary work and many other kinds of work. You will find opportunities in the more regularly visited countries of Europe such as France and Italy, and the more unusual destinations in South America, Africa and Asia.

So just take your pick. Whatever kind of cultural experience you are looking for, you are sure to find it in *Working Holidays Abroad*. This book contains all the basic information you need to plan and organise your working holiday. In a few short weeks from now, you may be setting off on the trip of a lifetime.

Bon voyage!

MARK HEMPSHELL

Chapter One

HOW TO GET THE BEST FROM YOUR TRIP

Tempting though it may be to just take off on your holiday, it cannot be emphasised strongly enough how important it is to do a little forward planning. Part of the fun of a working holiday is that you get to see and do things you would not be able to on an ordinary paid-for holiday, and it would be a shame not to get as much out of your travels as you can. Sure, you can change plans enroute, but it is essential to set down some ground rules before you make the final decision to go.

It is a good idea to write down your priorities, especially if you travel with friends. Each of you will have your own ideas of what to see or where to go, so make separate lists and compare notes.

ASK YOURSELF THESE QUESTIONS

Do you just have a two-week break in mind? Or do you have a year off? Maybe you are in the very fortunate position of being able to travel for as long as you like and only return home when you are bored with being away? Remember, travelling off the beaten track takes time. You can zip around Europe in a fortnight but it takes much longer to cover Africa or the U.S.A. fairly extensively.

Where to go? So much choice, so many places... the only way to decide properly is to make a list of the places you want to visit and rank them in order of priority. You can save a great deal of money on travel by moving around the world in roughly the same direction, rather than back-tracking time and again. You may not be able to see everything, so do not be too ambitious. But if you have always wanted to see Athens or the Great Wall of China, make sure they go down on your itinerary.

What to do? If you are looking forward to working as you travel, remember that the work available varies from country to country, and from town to town. There are not many opportunities, for example, to work as a ski guide in Africa or teach English in England, and China is one of the countries in which there are few opportunities to earn much money.

Fortunately, there is a solution: if you want to visit a place where there may not be many work opportunities, you can work (and save) like crazy in another location to pay for your trip. For example, you may dislike the hustle and bustle of Hong Kong but there is good money to be earned there which will pay for a few weeks' well-deserved holiday in China.

SAMPLE ITINERARIES

Here are some ideas for your working trip:

ITINERARY 1

This trip around Europe by road took Ian McGregor 12 months:

February-April

Worked as a courier with a skiing holiday company in Davos, Switzerland.

April-September

Hitchhiked down to Athens and caught a ferry to the Greek isles. Moved around a couple of islands and finally found a job as a barman-cum-general assistant in a bar on the Greek island of Kos.

October

Took a ferry back to Athens and did casual fruit-picking on the Greek mainland.

November-January

Bought a rail ticket home but stopped off on the way and found a job over Christmas in a bar in the southern German city of Munich.

13

ITINERARY 2

A trip to some Asian countries which took Janet Stephens nine months:

February-May

Arrived in Hong Kong to work as a journalist with one of its English-language newspapers. Worked two evenings a week in a bar for extra money.

May-June

Flew to Bangkok, Thailand, and found a couple of weeks' work in a language school teaching English. Spent two weeks touring Thailand before travelling by rail through Malaysia to Singapore. Spent a short holiday there, then took a flight to Tokyo.

July-September

Arrived in Japan and took a job as an English teacher in a private language school. Also worked in the evenings as a private English teacher.

October

Travelled back home to the United Kingdom, stopping off in San Francisco and New York for a holiday along the way.

ITINERARY 3

*This working holiday in Spain and France took Andrew Jones
and Tom Fielding eight weeks:*

June

Took a cheap flight to Spain's Costa del Sol. Found work in a hotel bar in the evenings.

July

Hitchhiked to the south of France. Spent four weeks doing odd jobs at a French campsite. Spent more time in the south of France before hitchhiking home to London through Paris.

ITINERARY 4

Mark Thomson spent 12 months on a working holiday in Australia:

April-June

Flew to Australia with a Working Holiday Visa. Took a casual job in the packing department of a factory in Sydney.

July-January

Took a coach trip to Melbourne. Found a job as a telephone sales assistant in an office.

January-February

Tired of the nine-to-five office routine. Resigned and hitchhiked into rural New South Wales. Found casual work picking apples.

March-April

Travelled overland to the Queensland coast. Found a few weeks' casual work in a hotel kitchen on the Gold Coast, then spent a few weeks lazing on the beach. Flew home when the visa expired.

ITINERARY 5

This trip took Alison Anderson and her friend about 20 weeks:

June-August

Took a cheap holiday flight to Turkey, hired a car and travelled around the busy holiday resorts on the southwest coast. Found casual work in a hotel cleaning the rooms and looking after the owner's children.

September

Spent two weeks in Bodrum.

September-October

Intended to go home but travelled to Istanbul instead. Found a job helping out in a nursery and managed to put in some sightseeing as well.

Hopefully, these sample itineraries will give you some ideas with which to plan your own. Just remember that there are no restrictions. You alone can decide where you want to go and what you want to do. If you head for Europe planning to work on a farm but end up looking after children in Cairo, or tending a bar counter in Turkey, look upon it as part of the fun. But, whatever you do, it is good to have some aims before you set out. They will make your trip more enjoyable.

MONEY MATTERS

You will have to face up to the fact that your holiday is going to cost you money, whether you find work or not. The costs vary in different parts of the world compared with what you are used to at home. Some countries are relatively cheap to visit and live in; others, a lot more expensive.

The Perils of Travelling Penniless: Is it possible to set off with absolutely nothing and pay for your travel solely by working? Well, it is, but such a move is not advisable. There are people who leave home with just small change in their pocket and still manage to see the world. But it is very risky. Besides, most countries refuse to admit travellers who do not have at least enough cash on them to pay for a few nights' accommodation and food.

You Need an Emergency Fund. To be on the safe side, you will need an emergency fund—some money to use when you are stuck in Stockholm at eleven at night, for example, with no work in sight—and you need somewhere to stay! If you are travelling in Europe, which tends to be the most expensive area of the world, an emergency fund of about US$2,000 is the minimum. Hopefully, you will not have to spend it, but it is good to have it there just in case.

Raising the Money. You should start planning the financial side of things as soon as you make the decision to go. Here are some of the ways you can raise the cash:

- Save, save, save! Save every penny or cent you can from now on.
- Get a second job. Look for a holiday or a part-time job now. It is always easier to get a job in your own country than abroad.
- Sell something. You will not be able to take your bike, car or stereo system on your working trip, so why not sell it? That way, the money can be put to work for you and not remain idle.
- Borrow from friends and relatives. It is well worth asking. At least, ask them for the cash to set up an emergency fund which, hopefully, you can repay when you get back.
- Call on your bank manager. You may not realise it but your bank may be willing to lend you the money for a working trip— especially if you have a job waiting for you when you return.

IF YOUR HOLIDAY IS A 'YEAR-BETWEEN'

You may be thinking of taking your working holiday as a year-between—before going off to college or university. And why not? You will never have a chance like this again. Besides, a lot of students find that they do much better in their course of study backed by some knowledge of the world around them. Here are some tips you will find useful:

- Make sure you will not mind returning to your academic studies. Once you have experienced a working holiday, it can be very difficult to pick those books up again.
- Secure your place in college before you leave. Many colleges and universities allow you to start your course the next year even if your original application is for the current year.
- If the work that you do during your holiday relates to your course of study, it may impress the college and will certainly impress your future employers.
- Make use of what contacts there may be at your future college or

university. They may have an employment or travel officer who is willing to help current as well as future students.

- Do not overestimate your skills. Even if you have secured a place in a prestigious course at a well-respected university, you may still find yourself washing dishes or cleaning floors during your working trip.

- Make plans to return home with plenty of time to spare. You will need at least six weeks to settle back into a routine and get ready for your course.
- Do not forget to return home. You will regret it later if you do not take up your planned course of study.

SOME DOS AND DON'TS

Before you go off and do your own thing—and that is part of the fun of a working holiday—here are additional tips:

- Always have an itinerary in mind. You can change it later but it is good to start out with definite plans.
- Set a date for your departure now so that you will have something to work towards.
- Travel with a friend, or friends, if you wish. It is a lot of fun and

much safer too, but remember that it is harder for two or three people to find a job in the same place than just one.

- Divide your destinations into working destinations (places where there is a good chance you will be able to get a job) and holiday destinations (where jobs are few and you may have to spend your cash reserves).
- Always take as much money as you can afford (at least enough to return home if you cannot find a job).
- Get as much information as possible about your destination before you arrive. If you can, line up a job before you go or take along the addresses of possible employers.
- Where possible, pre-book your accommodation for your first night in a new city.
- Check passports and visas before you go. It is usually too late once you arrive at the border.
- Do not write to employers if you can telephone them or knock on their door. This is probably the best piece of advice you can get.
- Stay clear of prospective employers who offer to pay you well to do something illegal—for example, drug smuggling!

The rest of this book focuses on the types of work available and the opportunities that exist all over the world.

Chapter Two

JOB OPPORTUNITIES AROUND THE WORLD

The nature of work you can do while travelling varies greatly, and you may want to look for a job for which you are particularly qualified or have the work experience. This section, however, looks at the types of work that are most frequently taken up by working travellers looking for cash and some fun.

JOBS IN AGRICULTURE

If you have ever spoken to a farmer, you will know that farms are always in need of casual help except, perhaps, in winter when there is not so much to do. Help is most sought after during busy seasons

JOB OPPORTUNITIES AROUND THE WORLD

such as planting or harvest.

If you work on a farm, you must be prepared to work long hours (such as from dawn to dusk, or even longer) and do anything and everything. This includes looking after animals, driving a tractor, planting, picking fruit or digging ditches.

Arranging a Job Before You Go. There are some organisations which can arrange farm placements before you leave. If you have some agricultural experience, the International Farm Experience Programme may be able to arrange a job for you. Or, if you are interested in organic farming, the Willing Workers on Organic Farms may be able to help. Addresses of these organisations in several countries are given in the directory listing in Chapter Five of this book.

How to Get a Job. If you do not already have a job lined up, you can refer to the newspapers or employment agencies upon your arrival, but it is usually worth heading for the nearest farms and introducing yourself. If you can drive, repair machinery or have any experience with animals, be sure to mention this to the farmer. Most of them are always very busy and do not have time to train new recruits.

Free Accommodation on Farms. If you intend to look for farm work during the summer, consider taking a tent along as farmers in most countries will let casual workers camp on their land, or in a barn or outhouse, for free. Some farmers will also throw in free food as part of your wages, so ask about this when discussing payment.

WORKING AS AN AU PAIR OR NANNY

This is one of the nicest ways of working abroad. It is usually open to young women between the ages of 17 and 27, although a few countries (such as the Scandinavian countries and, sometimes, Germany, France and the U.S.A.) employ male au pairs. Do ask if you are interested. Your work will involve looking after children and helping around the house with light duties such as cleaning, washing

23

and cooking, but you should not be expected to work as a maid.

Au pairs receive free food and accommodation in the family home, as well as a small wage. In some countries, au pairs are expected to take up a local language or arts course, but you should also be given plenty of free time as well. This can be a good way of working abroad if you do not want to be totally independent.

What Does a Nanny Do? Nannies are paid a proper wage but may not necessarily be provided with accommodation in the family home. Nannying work is available to women of any age.

How to Find a Job. You should apply to employment agencies which specialise in this type of work (many addresses are given in the directory listing of this book) or look up newspaper advertisements when you arrive abroad (details of newspapers in foreign countries are also given in the directory). If you go through a good agency, you can expect to receive a fair wage, be provided with health insurance and free travel to your job, and find placement with a family whose background has been established by the agency.

Are There Any Drawbacks? One snag with working as an au pair is that you may have to commit yourself for a minimum period, such as three or six months, or even up to a year. This may not be the ideal type of work if you do not want a fairly long commitment, or if you think you may get homesick once you arrive abroad.

JOBS IN CHILDREN'S CAMPS

There are summer camps for children in many countries. These are found in the U.S.A. and some European countries such as France. The jobs involved are as monitors, counsellors, instructors and backup staff including cooks, drivers and maintenance people.

To get such work, you must usually be below 30. It helps if you have a special skill, such as being able to teach a sport, and a certificate to prove it. You must also like working with children or your working holiday will turn into a nightmare if you have to cope with a bunch of rowdy kids day after day.

How to Get a Job. This type of work is available in summer only, so you must plan ahead and arrange it in advance, if possible. Write to the organisation which runs the camp as early as six months before it is due to start (that is, during the previous winter). Some addresses are listed in Chapter Five.

CONSERVATION WORK

This is the sort of work which will appeal to you if you are interested in looking after the planet. Most countries have conservation projects of one kind or another and there are lots of opportunities to get involved. The jobs are varied and include archaeology, preserving wildlife habitats, restoring historic property, building footpaths, caring for trees and clearing waterways. In fact, there is bound to be something to suit everyone.

How to Get a Job. You must have a genuine interest in such work and be prepared to get involved no matter how dirty or hard the job may be. It also helps if you have some previous experience or skills— for example, archaeology or gardening—that can be used.

The disadvantage is that such work does not offer much pay, if any. However, you can usually expect free food and accommodation and probably receive a small wage. This gives you plenty of opportunity to travel to places and do things you would not normally be able to do.

The best way to secure such work is to apply to one of the voluntary agencies which work in the field of conservation. There are many listed in the directory in Chapter Five.

JOBS IN CONSTRUCTION

Opportunities include work on building sites, and road building or repair. If you have any experience, so much the better but if you do not, you may be taken on as a labourer or general assistant.

Finding a Job. Visit local building sites and the local office of the national employment service (addresses in the directory). One point: you must apply very early in the morning (5 a.m.–7 a.m.) as work starts early, especially in countries with a warm climate.

Beware! Safety standards are much lower in some countries than in others. If you turn up at a construction site only to find extremely low safety standards, it may be better to look elsewhere.

DOMESTIC WORK

In many countries, there is a high demand for people who are willing to take on domestic chores. The work is hard and sometimes dirty, but the advantage is that you do not need any sort of experience or special skill. You may find yourself working as a maid or cleaner; doing the laundry, gardening or shopping; or looking after the children—often all at the same time.

How to Get a Job. Try local employment agencies and newspapers. You can also consider placing a newspaper advertisement under the 'Work Wanted' heading once you arrive, or go knocking on doors. Schools and nurseries are often a good place to meet busy mothers who need a little help around the house.

The Pay. This ranges from low to fairly high, especially in wealthier countries such as Germany and Switzerland. You may even be provided with accommodation for some jobs. Whatever you do, make sure your wages are fair and that you get reasonable time off.

JOBS IN BARS

Bar work has often been the life-saver of working travellers the world over. Wherever you go, you can almost certainly count on being recruited for serving, waiting or washing up in bars, cafes, pubs, inns and other such establishments. The only setback is that, during busy times, there can sometimes be more workers than jobs available. The pay may be low but you can sometimes get free food and accommodation thrown in, and you may be able to earn more money from tips.

Good Advice. It is often pointless to line up bar work in advance. Simply call or drop in when you get there. Look for 'Staff Wanted' or 'Help Wanted' notices but do not be put off if there are none—just knock on the door and ask.

Be Warned! Women usually find bar work much easier to obtain than men. Rightly or wrongly, bar owners the world over aim to attract their male customers with a pretty face. As such, it is wise to be on the lookout for unscrupulous bar owners who advertise for female bar staff or dancers, but expect them to become involved in prostitution. Try and establish that the bar is genuine before you apply and if you are not happy with the job on the first day, leave immediately.

JOBS IN HOTELS AND RESTAURANTS

Hotels and restaurants offer some of the best opportunities for working travellers as they are always in need of casual staff to help out at busy times or during their peak season (which varies in different parts of the world).

What are You Expected to Do? Most hotels and restaurants have opportunities for people without previous experience. The most common types of work are those of waiter, kitchen porter, chambermaid, bar staff, porter or bell boy. If you can speak the local language, you may be able to do reception or concierge work.

Having some experience in hotel or restaurant work always makes it easier for you to find a job abroad, so you may want to consider taking on a part-time hotel or restaurant job in your own country before you leave on your working holiday.

How to Get a Job. Try private employment agencies or the local office of the national employment service, but you should also visit the local hotels or restaurants personally. Ask to see the owner or manager. You can also write to such places before you begin your holiday. If you can speak any foreign languages, be sure to say so as it will increase your chances of being employed.

Free Accommodation. One advantage is that accommodation is often available on the premises, plus as much food as you can eat. However, they may not necessarily be provided free, so check what costs are involved before accepting the job. Occasionally, some unscrupulous employers overcharge their staff for accommodation.

JOBS ON A KIBBUTZ

A kibbutz is a collective farm most commonly found in Israel. Members of a kibbutz earn no wages, but work together for the common good and are provided with all their basic living necessities. A moshav operates in a similar way, but is a group of independent farmers working together. The concept also operates in some other countries, but under a different name.

Kibbutzim (the plural of kibbutz) welcome foreign volunteers to join them and share their lifestyle for a few months. The work can be hard and involve long hours, and duties may include farm work (sowing, harvesting and animal care), childcare, cleaning and maintenance. A kibbutz will provide accommodation and a small wage, whereas moshavim pay full wages.

How to Get a Job. Although it is possible to apply directly to a kibbutz, it is generally easier to apply through an agency. Details of agencies in Israel and other countries are found in the directory section.

JOBS IN SHOPS OR OFFICES

Wherever there are shops and offices, there are bound to be jobs available as these places need temporary and part-time staff to help out at busy times. The work is varied—shop assistant, cashier, stock room assistant, warehouse assistant, clerk, typist, receptionist, office attendant or mail room assistant—and the sort of job you may land depends on what you can and want to do.

The Drawbacks. You will often need a knowledge of the local language if it is not English, or you may be unable to do the work.

How to Get a Job. Apply through employment agencies or look up newspaper advertisements. Many contacts are given in the directory section. Alternatively, you can try telephoning or dropping by at shops and offices and asking if they need help for a few days or weeks. Make sure you are smartly dressed. The pay tends to be better than what you will receive for casual jobs, and you may even be hired for a few months if you want to remain that long.

JOBS AT SEA

Unless you have relevant experience, it is not too easy these days to get a job on a tanker, freighter or fishing vessel. Modern ships are highly automated, requiring only a handful of staff who usually have specialist knowledge and qualifications. However, do not give up hope if you are dreaming of spending time on the ocean waves, as there are still some non-technical openings.

Working on a Cruise Ship. More and more cruise ships are taking to the oceans every year and a single ship carries several hundred crew. All the ships have regular vacancies, particularly for waiters, bar staff, stewards, cleaners, kitchen staff, sports instructors, entertainers, hairdressers and the like.

If you are interested in working on a cruise ship, bear in mind that the cruise lines prefer those with the experience of doing the job on dry land. You will increase your chances of finding a job if you get the necessary experience before you leave.

To get this kind of work, apply to the cruise lines or employment agencies well in advance. If you cannot do so, check if vacancies are available by calling on the cruise ships when they arrive in port.

Working on Private Yachts. The opportunities range from working on a luxury super-yacht owned by a multi-millionaire to a charter yacht with holidaymakers sailing for a couple of weeks in summer. Countries such as France, Spain, Greece, Turkey and many Asian and Caribbean countries have these opportunities. Your work may be that of cook, cleaner, maintenance hand or deckhand.

To get such jobs on board private vessels, you can try the local employment agencies but it is easy enough to go down to the harbour and approach the yacht owners directly.

JOBS IN TEACHING

In many countries, it is possible to find work as a language teacher even if you have no experience or teaching qualifications. Your main selling point would be your ability to speak English, and this is especially so if it is your native language.

In many countries, especially those in southern Europe, South America and Asia, English speakers are hired to give language lessons to the locals. This usually involves conversational practice only, which is why no special skills are required. The teaching of English is among the most highly paid casual work you can find.

How to Get a Job. Contact language school employment agencies and the schools themselves. Watch out, too, for advertisements in the newspapers. You can also find many addresses in the directory section of this book.

Your chances of finding a job will be greatly increased if you take a short Teaching English as a Foreign Language (TEFL) course before you leave home. Details of courses are available from your local colleges and universities, and also from The English Language Information Unit, The British Council, 10 Spring Gardens, London, SW1A 2BN, U.K.

JOBS IN TOURISM

Wherever there are tourists, there are also opportunities for work. In addition to hotels, restaurants and bars, work opportunities exist in nightclubs, discos, theme parks, zoos, water parks, resort shops and where sports facilities (such as yacht clubs) are available.

What Jobs Are Available? These include work as holiday representatives, camp couriers, chalet maids, maintenance persons and entertainers (singers, dancers and musicians), as well as work in public relations, promoting facilities such as bars and restaurants. If you are a determined person, you may even find yourself selling refreshments on the beach, if not selling holiday villas and apartments.

How to Find a Job. The best way is to approach the local employment agencies, or write to or call on employers directly. Many useful addresses are given later in this book. If you can, apply well in advance of the season. Employers always need a minimum number of staff and will appoint them in advance, although others will also be hired on the spot depending on the numbers of tourists who turn up in that year.

Bear in Mind. The tourist season varies around the world. Summer is the most popular time in the Mediterranean resorts in Europe but in the skiing industry in the Alps, the main source of employment is in winter. In the southern hemisphere, such as Australia, the tourist season is from October to March.

A Snag to Consider. Tourism-related work is available only where there are tourists so if you want to get off the tourist track and see some of the 'real' culture of the country, you will have to find some other work.

JOBS ON VOLUNTARY PROJECTS

You may think that voluntary work is never paid for but, like work in conservation projects, this is not always the case. Although most voluntary work is done free, some projects do pay a small sum of 'pocket money'. At the very least, though, you should receive free food and accommodation, which can be worth quite a sum.

In any case, doing some sort of voluntary work can be worthwhile. It can also be a good way of really getting involved with a foreign country and its people, and seeing things that tourists rarely see.

Opportunities That Exist. The range is wide and includes working with children and the poor, elderly or disabled, or there may be work in schools, hospitals, hostels and community centres. The work is often physically and mentally demanding so you must be fit and prepared to dig in and do a bit of everything.

The best way to find voluntary work is to apply to a voluntary agency or charity before you leave home. Lots of addresses are given later and you are advised to write and ask for details of the latest projects—at least three months in advance, if possible. It can be quite difficult to find work on voluntary projects once you have arrived abroad.

NOTHING THAT INTERESTS?
THEN USE YOUR IMAGINATION!

The above are areas in which work is most commonly available. However, do not let it restrict your plans. If you travel abroad with an open mind and are prepared to do anything, your trip will be much more successful—and so much more exciting too.

Many useful contact addresses which may lead to many other types of work are given in Chapter Five. So use the leads provided, coupled with your own imagination, to find work you really enjoy. If you are travelling in the United States and hear about an opportunity to act in a film, or passing through Poland and discover an opportunity to work in a circus, why not explore them further? One of them could just be the job for you.

Useful advice. Most countries, with few exceptions, have a problem with unemployment and you will be competing with the local people for many of the jobs. If you do not speak any or much of the local language, your chance of employment will be ranked lower than that of the locals. The best advice, therefore, is that you need to be determined and flexible if you are to make a success of your trip.

Whether or not you can legally take on any jobs in the countries of your choice depends on the local law on visas and work permits. More advice is given in Chapters Three and Five.

THINGS TO WATCH OUT FOR

Beware of unscrupulous employers and dubious work schemes. As you travel looking for work, you are sure to meet many other travellers who are keen to work as well. Unfortunately, you may also encounter some employers who are equally keen to take advantage of this small army of people wishing to work to fund their travel.

The majority of employers are honest but you should be on your guard when trying to secure work in an unfamiliar country. Here are some traps to look out for:

- Agencies that charge you fees to find a job. Genuine agencies

33

(with the exception of charities and au pair agencies) do not usually charge the employee any fees because these are paid for by the employer.

- Agencies that offer you a job if you pay for a flight or coach trip to the destination country. Often, there is no genuine job on arrival.
- Employers who advertise jobs which turn out to be something else. For example, women hired as barmaids or hostesses may be expected to work as prostitutes.
- Employers who overcharge for food, accommodation, social security or tax.
- Employers who do not pay you at the end of the week or month.
- Employers who offer to pay you well to do something that is illegal, for example, drug smuggling.

As long as you are aware of all the problems and pitfalls involved, there is no need to worry unduly. But if, at any time, you are not happy about a job offer, then simply go elsewhere. There will always be something else to do, in some other part of the world.

Chapter Three

PLANNING A SAFE AND ENJOYABLE TRIP

TRIGG

In this chapter, some basic requirements are addressed.

HOW TO FIND ACCOMMODATION THAT IS CHEAP AND GOOD

Plan ahead! You are going to need somewhere to stay, even if all you do is sleep there. The cost of accommodation varies considerably around the world, from very cheap to very expensive. There is also a shortage of accommodation in some countries—mainly those popular with tourists and working travellers.

Make plans in advance wherever possible but book your accommodation for the first night or two only before leaving home. It is usually easier to scout around for more reasonable prices when you arrive. Also, once you know how long you will be staying, you can choose the type of accommodation that suits your requirements best.

Youth Hostels. These are the working travellers' best friend. You can find them in almost every country and they can generally be relied on to offer reliable accommodation at a fair price. They can usually be used by people of all ages, although those below the age of 25 get priority at busy times. Even if you do not want to stay in a hostel for too long (most impose a maximum period of stay, anyway) it is an ideal place to set up base until you find your feet in a new town.

Many youth hostels belong to the International Youth Hostel Federation (IYHF). The IYHF in each country can tell you about the many hostels it operates in the various parts of that country, together with booking conditions and costs. Once you have joined the IYHF in your own country, you can stay in any IYHF hostel worldwide.

There are also privately run hostels in most countries, although the standard of these varies. If you cannot find a hostel on arrival, ask at tourist information offices, on university campuses or even at a police station.

It is worth remembering that many IYHF member organisations have a travel office, either in the hostel or nearby. The travel office can help you locate more permanent accommodation, make further travel arrangements and, more often than not, obtain discounts for you on air, rail and coach tickets. These can be worth up to 30% off in some cases, so it is worth asking, even if you are not staying in the hostel.

Finally, many youth hostels have staff who know about local job vacancies. Many of them even have a notice board where employers put up casual advertisements looking for working travellers to fill vacant posts. All this is carried out on an unofficial basis—it is not really the job of the hostel—and offers another good reason why you should drop in on youth hostels when you are travelling abroad.

Hotels. The word 'hotel' covers a wide range of accommodation, from luxury-grade establishments to hostels. Inns and pensions (boarding houses) are also hotels. Even if you are travelling on a tight budget, a hotel is not necessarily out of your reach if you bargain hard. There are lots of ways you can save money and get a pleasant room for less than the standard rate.

- Always ask for a discount. This is expected in many countries.
- Never walk into a hotel and pay the going rate. Telephone first if possible.
- Avoid booking through national booking offices. (They ask for top rates.)
- Note that in some countries, like the U.S.A., charges are on a per-room and not per-person basis. Sharing can reduce the cost considerably.
- Make use of discount cards and promotional offers in newspapers.
- Ask if there is a price 'without breakfast'—you can often save up to 30% or 40% of the bill.

Guest Houses and Private Rooms. These can be found in many parts of the world. They are always cheaper than hotels but the facilities are often as good, if not better. Often, they are cheap enough to stay in for quite a long while and a good idea in places such as Japan or Switzerland, where it is just too expensive to rent an apartment.

The main snag is finding out where the guest houses are because they rarely advertise. Many tourist offices publish a list, so write ahead of your journey and ask for a list of guest houses or rooms in the area you will be visiting.

Campsites. Camping is the cheapest accommodation you are likely to find anywhere and is ideal for a short stay. The setback is that it is usually available only in summer, and a tent is not a very secure place in which to keep your valuables. If you are looking for a job, prospective employers will not be impressed by a campsite address because it gives the impression that you do not intend to stay long.

Get details of campsites in advance from a tour guide or tourist office. If you camp away from an official site, always get the landowner's permission. It is not a good idea to camp on public land as it is illegal in many countries. Many IYHF hostels, by the way, allow camping in the grounds free, or for a small fee.

Live-in Accommodation. Some jobs offer live-in accommodation. This often applies to jobs in hotels or catering. Living in can be very convenient, especially if shifts or late-night work are involved. But there can be drawbacks: live-in accommodation is sometimes not of a very good standard and some employers charge more than it is really worth. Always ask what the charges are for staff quarters, then look up the local newspapers and check what you would otherwise have to pay for a flat or hotel room. Settle on the live-in accommodation only if you think that the charges are fair. Do this before you accept the job and move your things in.

Renting an Apartment. If you are going to stay in a place for some time, you can consider renting a house or apartment. It will work out cheaper in the long run but you may have to commit yourself to a minimum lease of six or 12 months.

Do not sign any lease until you have inspected the property, which means that you cannot confirm your accommodation until you arrive at your destination. To locate suitable property, look in the local newspapers or go to a property agent, but bear in mind that an agent may charge you a fee.

Usually, you will need to place a cash bond (from which the landlord will deduct any damage you may cause) and pay rent in advance. Ask about any extra charges—in some countries, for example, it is usual for the landlord to charge for heating, hot water, insurance and the cleaning of communal areas in addition to the rent.

If you cannot afford an apartment of your own, sharing is a good idea. In some countries, there are agents who will arrange this for you. In Germany, for example, there is Mitwohnzentrale, an agency that makes the flat-sharing arrangement, or *wohngemeinschaften*, for you.

Other Kinds of Cheap or Free Accommodation. If you are determined (or short of cash), you can stretch your money further by really using your imagination when it comes to accommodation. For example, some working travellers, especially in remote areas, have been known to knock on the nearest door and ask for shelter for the night. In countries where people are traditionally very hospitable and the crime rate is low, it is by no means unusual. In other countries, police stations may give a bed for the night to travellers who cannot find or afford anything else.

39

In some countries, charity hostels are willing to take in any traveller, and not just the homeless. In others, churches, temples, convents and monasteries will take in those who are passing through, either for free or in return for a small donation. For instance, the guest dormitory at Po Lin Monastery on Lantau Island, Hong Kong, is a popular retreat for travellers wanting to spend some time away from the bustle of the city.

Since information about these cheap or free sources of accommodation is rarely, if ever, published, you will need to keep your ear to the ground. Make a point of talking to any other working travellers whom you encounter at airports, railway and bus stations, and in other public places. You can usually find out about some cheap and unusual places in which to stay.

HOW TO AVOID GETTING INTO TROUBLE WITH CUSTOMS

Before you leave home, be sure to get the relevant Customs information for all the countries you want to visit. This can be obtained from embassies and consulates, or tourist offices. These are the things you need to know:

- Is there any limit on the amount of personal possessions which can be taken into your destination country? Some countries limit these according to their value.
- Do you need a permit for anything? A few countries do not allow items such as bicycles, cameras, gold, videos or even books to be imported without a permit.
- Are there any items that are totally banned? For example, with a few exceptions, you must not try to take foodstuffs into the U.S.A.
- If you take any drug or medication, it is vital to check if it is permitted. It may be legal in your country, but illegal in your destination country.
- Never be tempted to smuggle illegal drugs from one country to another. Most countries take this matter very seriously and impose

long prison sentences on offenders. Some countries impose the death penalty for those caught smuggling even small quantities of illegal drugs.

Always think and plan ahead. It is too late when you are checking in for your flight to your next destination.

INSURANCE—THE COVERAGE YOU NEED

It is essential to take out insurance cover before you travel. You are more likely to encounter some mishap when travelling in a strange culture than when you are in familiar surroundings and if the worst does happen, the proper insurance protection can help prevent a complete financial disaster. This is what you need to be covered for:

- **Health.** Not many countries offer free medical treatment to foreign visitors. There are some exceptions (such as if you are a citizen of an EU (European Union) country travelling in another) but you should usually make your own arrangements. The costs of medical treatment is high in most places and you should take at least US$1 million cover worldwide or US$2 million if travelling to the U.S.A. Make sure you are covered for hospital treatment, drugs and repatriation (a flight home if your illness cannot be treated on the spot).
- **Personal Accident.** This will provide cash to cover your expenses if you meet with a road accident, are injured while playing a sport, or even if you just fall in the street.
- **Luggage and Personal Possessions.** These have to be covered against loss, theft and damage.
- **Personal Liability and Legal Expenses.** This will pay for a lawyer if you are arrested by the police.

Insurance is usually cheaper (and easier to arrange) if you take it out in your home country, rather than when you are travelling. Always go directly to an insurance company, rather than a travel agent. If you are a student, be sure to say so as discounts are often offered. When taking out insurance, tell your insurance company

41

that you plan to work. If you do not, you may find that you are not covered for accidents or illness which occur when you are at work.

STAYING HEALTHY DURING YOUR TRIP

Before leaving home, call on your doctor, dentist and optician for a check-up. Tell them where you are going and what you will be doing. It is better to take advice from a doctor who knows you, rather than a stranger abroad who may not even speak your language.

If you are taking any medication, arrange for a supply to be sent to you abroad if necessary. Your doctor can arrange for a friend or relative to collect your usual prescription and provide a letter to travel with the drugs, stating what they are and what they are for. This will avoid any problems at Customs.

Getting Medical Treatment Abroad. The most important thing to remember is that you cannot usually get free medical treatment abroad. Even if you are already protected by medical insurance, it will probably not cover you while you are working in a foreign country, so you must make sure you have medical insurance specifically for your trip.

A few countries have reciprocal agreements with one another but this is the exception rather than the rule. If you are a citizen of an EU country travelling to another EU country, you can get some free medical treatment there. To claim the benefit, pick up Form E111 from your nearest post office or social security office and take it with you on your trip. The EU countries are Austria, Belgium, Denmark, Finland, France, Germany, Greece, Ireland, Italy, Luxembourg, Netherlands, Portugal, Spain, Sweden and the U.K.

Health Risks. Before leaving home check the state of public health in the countries you intend to visit. General information can be found in a book called the ABC *Guide to International Travel,* which many travel agents and libraries have.

If you live in the U.S.A. you can contact the U.S. Public Health Service Center for Disease Control on tel. 404 332 4559 for health advice. If you live in Europe, you can contact The Medical Advisory Service to Travellers Abroad (MASTA), Keppel Street, London, U.K., tel. 0171 631 4408.

Check in particular if the countries you intend to visit present a risk of cholera, polio, yellow fever, typhoid or hepatitis A. If so, you will need to arrange a course of vaccinations with your local doctor or clinic. Ideally, you should make these arrangements at least 12 weeks before departure as some courses of treatment need time to take effect.

In countries where infectious diseases may be caught, few demand that visitors get themselves vaccinated beforehand, but often advise in favour of it. In any case, it is best to get your vaccinations before leaving home as you can budget for the cost better and make sure they are carried out in hygienic conditions. Remember to take the vaccination certificates with you when you travel.

If you are travelling to an area where malaria-carrying mosquitoes are a problem, you may need anti-malaria tablets. Usually, you will have to start taking them at least two weeks before leaving. The dosage and type of tablets depend on where you are going; Chloroquine is the main drug but it is not suitable for all destinations. Besides medication, you should also take precautions against insect bites. Use an insect repellent spray and take a mosquito net if there is a chance that you will be sleeping in the open or in rooms that are not screened.

The chart on the following pages shows what precautions are usually advised for travellers. However, since the situation is liable to change and the exact vaccinations that you will need depend on your country of origin, you should check the situation with your own doctor or clinic.

Another health risk is that of AIDS. It is present in most countries nowadays, although the extent of the disease and the risk of catching it varies from slight to considerable depending on the place you are travelling to. The main risks of catching AIDS occur after sexual contact with an infected person, or treatment using medical equipment that has not been properly sterilised. You cannot catch the AIDS virus from food, drink or insect bites.

You can minimise the risk of contracting this fatal disease by minimising sexual contact and using a condom. Use the facilities of hospitals, clinics and dentists that observe a high standard of hygiene; if the premises look dirty, the chances are that the medical equipment is too. If you are visiting a country where the standard of medical treatment is questionable, it is worth taking your own sterile medical kit of needles, syringes and dressings. These can be bought from travel suppliers. They usually contain a letter in various languages to inform Customs that they are for legitimate uses.

VACCINATIONS THAT MAY BE REQUIRED

Destination	Cholera	Yellow Fever	Typhoid Polio Hepatitis A	Malaria*
Afghanistan	Y	Y	R	Y
Albania	N	N	N	N
Algeria	N	N	R	R
Angola	Y	Y	R	R
Argentina	N	N	R	R
Australia	N	N	N	N
Austria	N	N	N	N
Azores	N	N	N	N
Bahamas	N	N	R	N
Bangladesh	Y	N	Y	R
Barbados	N	N	R	N
Belgium	N	N	N	N
Bahrain	R	Y	R	R
Benin	Y	Y	Y	R
Bermuda	N	N	N	N
Bolivia	N	Y	R	R
Brazil	N	Y	Y	R
Brunei	Y	N	Y	N
Bulgaria	N	N	N	N
Burma (Myanmar)	Y	Y	Y	R
Burundi	Y	Y	Y	Y
Cambodia	R	N	R	R
Cameroon	Y	Y	Y	Y
Canada	N	N	N	N
Cape Verde	N	Y	Y	Y
Chad	Y	Y	Y	Y
Chile	N	N	N	N

China	R	Y	Y	R
Colombia	N	R	Y	R
Congo	Y	Y	Y	Y
Costa Rica	N	N	R	R
Côte d'Ivoire	Y	Y	Y	Y
Cuba	N	N	R	N
Cyprus	N	N	R	N
Czech Republic	N	N	N	N
Denmark	N	N	N	N
Djibouti	Y	Y	Y	Y
Dominica	N	N	R	N
Dominican Rep.	N	N	Y	Y
Ecuador	N	Y	Y	Y
Egypt	Y	N	Y	R
El Salvador	N	N	Y	Y
Ethiopia	Y	Y	Y	Y
Fiji	N	N	Y	N
Finland	N	N	N	N
France	N	N	N	N
Gabon	Y	Y	Y	Y
Gambia	Y	Y	Y	Y
Germany	N	N	N	N
Ghana	Y	Y	Y	Y
Gibraltar	N	N	N	N
Greece	N	N	N	N
Greenland	N	N	N	N
Grenada	N	N	Y	N
Guatemala	N	N	Y	Y
Guinea	Y	Y	Y	Y
Guinea-Bissau	Y	Y	Y	Y
Guyana	N	N	Y	Y
Haiti	N	N	Y	Y
Honduras	N	N	Y	Y

Hong Kong	N	N	Y	N
Hungary	N	N	N	N
Iceland	N	N	N	N
India	Y	Y	Y	Y
Indonesia	Y	N	Y	Y
Iran	Y	N	Y	Y
Iraq	Y	N	Y	R
Ireland	N	N	N	N
Israel	N	N	Y	N
Italy	N	N	N	N
Jamaica	N	N	Y	N
Japan	N	N	Y	N
Jordan	Y	N	Y	N
Kenya	Y	Y	Y	Y
Kiribati	N	N	Y	N
Korea	Y	N	Y	N
Kuwait	Y	N	Y	N
Laos	Y	Y	Y	Y
Lebanon	Y	N	Y	N
Liberia	Y	Y	Y	Y
Libya	Y	Y	Y	R
Luxembourg	N	N	N	N
Madagascar	Y	Y	Y	Y
Malawi	Y	N	Y	Y
Malaysia	Y	Y	Y	R
Maldives	R	N	Y	N
Mali	Y	Y	Y	Y
Mauritania	Y	Y	Y	Y
Mauritius	N	Y	Y	R
Mexico	N	N	Y	R
Morocco	Y	N	Y	R
Mozambique	Y	N	Y	Y
Namibia	Y	Y	Y	Y

47

Nepal	Y	N	Y	Y
Netherlands	N	N	N	N
New Caledonia	N	N	Y	N
New Zealand	N	N	N	N
Nicaragua	N	N	Y	Y
Niger	Y	Y	Y	Y
Nigeria	Y	Y	Y	Y
Norway	N	N	N	N
Oman	Y	N	Y	Y
Pakistan	Y	N	Y	Y
Panama	N	R	Y	R
Papua				
New Guinea	Y	N	Y	Y
Paraguay	N	N	Y	R
Peru	Y	Y	Y	R
Philippines	Y	N	Y	R
Poland	N	N	N	N
Portugal	N	N	N	N
Puerto Rico	N	N	Y	N
Qatar	Y	N	Y	N
Romania	N	N	N	N
Rwanda	Y	Y	Y	Y
Saint Lucia	N	N	Y	N
St.Vincent				
& Grenadines	N	N	Y	N
Saudi Arabia	Y	N	Y	R
Seychelles	N	N	Y	N
Sierra Leone	Y	Y	Y	Y
Singapore	Y	N	Y	N
Somalia	Y	Y	Y	Y
South Africa	Y	N	Y	R
Spain	N	N	N	N
Sri Lanka	Y	N	Y	Y

Sudan	Y	Y	Y	Y
Suriname	N	Y	Y	Y
Sweden	N	N	N	N
Switzerland	N	N	N	N
Syria	Y	N	Y	Y
Taiwan	Y	N	Y	N
Tanzania	Y	Y	Y	Y
Thailand	Y	N	Y	Y
Togo	Y	Y	Y	Y
Tonga	N	N	Y	N
Trinidad & Tobago	N	N	Y	N
Tunisia	Y	N	Y	N
Turkey	N	N	Y	R
Uganda	Y	Y	Y	Y
U.A.E.	Y	N	Y	R
U.K.	N	N	N	N
U.S.A.	N	N	N	N
Former USSR	N	N	R	R
Uruguay	N	N	Y	N
Vanuatu	N	N	Y	Y
Venezuela	N	Y	Y	R
Vietnam	Y	N	Y	Y
Virgin Islands	N	N	Y	N
Yemen	Y	N	Y	Y
Zaire (Dem. Rep. of the Congo)	Y	Y	Y	Y
Zambia	Y	Y	Y	Y
Zimbabwe	Y	N	Y	Y

KEY TO CHART

Y   *Yes, vaccination is essential.*

N   *No, vaccination is not necessary.*

R   *Vaccination is not usually required but often recommended.*

*   *Protection against malaria is achieved by taking malaria tablets, not through vaccination.*

A cholera vaccination is not normally required for health reasons unless you will be in close contact with the local population in over-populated areas with poor sanitation. However, a few governments require that you be vaccinated. It is usually a good move to have tetanus vaccination at the same time as your other vaccinations because this disease is present in most countries. Ask your doctor if you are in doubt.

LEARNING A FOREIGN LANGUAGE

When travelling abroad, it is easy to forget that, although many people around the world speak English, the vast majority do not. While this is a minor problem if you are travelling on holiday, it becomes a major problem if you want to work.

The fact is, if you do not speak the local language, it will be much harder to get a job than if you do. Even if the locals do speak English as a second language, they may not want to and, in their own country, why should they?

You will increase your chances of finding work if you make an effort to learn some of the local language before you travel to a new country. Here are some of the ways you can learn:

- Audio-cassette courses—these can be costly and are often made for the holidaymaker, not the worker. You can save money by looking for second-hand courses advertised in the classified columns of newspapers.
- Evening classes—check with your local adult education colleges. Again, these courses are often aimed at the holidaymaker but they are fairly cheap.
- Commercial schools—an immersion course at a commercial language school is the fastest way to learn. It can be expensive, though. The Berlitz organisation runs schools in many countries, catering for most languages. You can get further details from their office at 9 Grosvenor Street, London, W1A 3BZ, U.K., tel. 0171 915 0909. Some countries run a language institute offering tuition at reasonable prices. For example, the French government runs the Institut Français network in several countries. Ask the embassy or consulate of the country you wish to visit for details.
- Summer schools—many universities run language courses in the summer and during vacations to make use of facilities which would otherwise be left idle. These courses are cheap and you often get the chance to practise with a native speaker. For example, many French universities run summer schools in French. For details, ask the embassy or consulate of the country you want to visit.

SOME PHRASES THAT MAY BE USEFUL

English **Good morning**
French *Bonjour*
German *Guten Morgen*
Italian *Buongiorno*
Spanish *Buenos Días*

English **Hello**
French *Bonjour*
German *Guten Tag*
Italian *Ciao*
Spanish *¡Hola!*

English **How are you?**
French *Comment-allez vous?*
German *Wie geht es Ihnen?*
Italian *Come sta?*
Spanish *Como esta?*

English **My name is ....**
French *Je m'appelle …*
German *Ich heiße …*
Italian *Mi chiamo …*
Spanish *Me llamo …*

English **Mr/Mrs/Miss**
French *Monsieur/Madame/Mademoiselle*
German *Herr/Frau/Fräulein*
Italian *Signore/Signora/Signora*
Spanish *Señor/Señora/Señorita*

English	**I am very pleased to meet you**
French	*Enchanté*
German	*Angenehm*
Italian	*Piacere. Leito di conoscerla*
Spanish	*Much gusto*

English	**Do you speak English?**
French	*Parlez vous anglais?*
German	*Sprechen Sie Englisch?*
Italian	*Parla Ingelese?*
Spanish	*Habla Ingles?*

English	**I don't speak ...**
French	*Je ne parle pas …*
German	*Ich spreche kein ….*
Italian	*Non parlo …*
Spanish	*No hablo …*

English	**I am ... years old**
French	*J'ai … ans.*
German	*Ich bien … jahre alt.*
Italian	*No … anni.*
Spanish	*Tengo … años.*

English	**Where is the ... ?**
French	*Où es …*
German	*Wo ist …*
Italian	*Dov'è …*
Spanish	*Dondé está ….?*

English	**Yes**
French	*Oui*
German	*Ja*
Italian	*Si*
Spanish	*Sí*

English	**No**
French	*Non*
German	*Nein*
Italian	*No*
Spanish	*No*

English	**Please**
French	*S'il vous plait*
German	*Bitte*
Italian	*Per favore*
Spanish	*Por favor*

English	**Thank you**
French	*Merci*
German	*Danke*
Italian	*Grazie*
Spanish	*Gracias*

English	**Goodbye**
French	*Au revoir*
German	*Auf Wiedersehen*
Italian	*Arrivederci!*
Spanish	*¡Adios!*

MONEY—HOW TO MAKE BOTH ENDS MEET WHILE YOU ARE AWAY

Whatever the amount of money you are able to take with you, it is a good idea to divide it into two lump sums: money with which to meet daily expenses and an emergency fund for unforeseen expenses such as accidents, missed trains or just ending up in a strange town with no possibility of finding a job.

The Best Way to Carry Money. Traveller's cheques are the best way of taking money with you. If they are lost or stolen, you can get a refund from the issuing company. U.S. dollar-cheques are the most widely accepted currency for your traveller's cheques: they can be changed in banks from Paris to Sydney, and from Moscow to Johannesburg. Surprisingly, U.S. banks do not usually change traveller's cheques, but most shops in the U.S. will accept them like cash and give you change too.

Travellers to EU (European Union) countries can take traveller's cheques in Euros and change them into the local currency at banks. However, notes and coins in the new all-Europe currency, the Euro, will not be issued until 2002.

Changing Money. Always shop around before exchanging cash and traveller's cheques abroad. Rates of exchange and exchange fees vary considerably between banks, hotel desks and change offices. In some countries, there are illegal moneychangers who offer more than the bank rate. They are best avoided because many are good at deception, especially where unsuspecting tourists are concerned.

Minimum Currency Requirements. To enter some countries, you must possess a minimum amount of money (in cash or traveller's cheques) before you will be allowed to cross the border. This is to make sure you have enough money to support yourself during your stay. Check that you have this money before departure. It is usually only a token amount and you may not be asked by the immigration officer to produce it but you should make sure you have it in hand. Some countries expect you to have an onward ticket (by air, rail or some other accepted means) before you are allowed to enter the country.

Local Bank Accounts. When staying in a country and working for more than a short period, it is usually worth opening a bank account in which to keep your money. Not only is it safer than carrying your cash around, but it also helps to establish your status and will, for example, help you to rent a place to live.

Currency Controls. Money can be imported and exported freely from and to many countries such as the U.K. and U.S.A. but other countries restrict currency movements. Usually, you must declare imports worth more than a certain amount to Customs upon entering, and get permission for exports above a certain value before leaving. How much the amount is varies from country to country.

The table on the following pages shows the currencies used by various countries and indicates which countries restrict currency imports and exports. Any bank will be able to give you up-to-date details of these restrictions.

COUNTRIES, CURRENCIES AND CURRENCY CONTROLS

Country	Currency (and Banker's Code)	Currency Controls?
Algeria	Dinar (ALD)	Y
Andorra	Franc/Peseta	N
Angola	Kwanza (AKZ)	Y
Anguilla	East Caribbean Dollar	N
Antigua & Barbuda	East Caribbean Dollar	N
Argentina	Austral (ARA)	N
Australia	Dollar (AUD)	N
Austria*	Schilling (AUS)	Y
Bahamas	Dollar (BMD)	Y
Bahrain	Dinar(BHD)	N
Bangladesh	Taka (BDT)	Y

Barbados	Dollar (BDD)	Y
Belgium*	Franc (BFR)	N
Belize	Dollar (BND)	Y
Benin	CFA Franc (CFA)	Y
Bermuda	Dollar (BMD)	N
Bolivia	Boliviano (BOB)	N
Botswana	Pula (BTP)	N
Brazil	Cruzado (BRZ)	N
Brunei	Dollar (B$)	Y
Bulgaria	Lev (LEV)	Y
Burma (Myanmar)	Kyat (BUR)	Y
Cameroon	CFA Franc	Y
Canada	Dollar (CAD)	N
Chad	CFA Franc	Y
Chile	Peso (CHP)	N
China	Renminbi (RMB)	Y
Colombia	Peso (COP)	Y
Comoro Islands	CFA Franc	N
Congo	CFA Franc	Y
Costa Rica	Colon (CRC)	N
Côte d'Ivoire	CFA Franc	Y
Cuba	Peso (CUP)	Y
Cyprus	Pound (CYL)	Y
Czech Republic	Koruna (CKR)	Y
Denmark	Krone (DKK)	Y
Dominica	Peso (DOP)	Y
Dominican Rep.	Sucre (SUC)	Y
Egypt	Pound (EGL)	Y
Ecuador	Colon (SAC)	N
Ethiopia	Birr (ETB)	Y
Fiji	Dollar (FID)	N
Finland*	Markka (FIM)	N
France*	Franc (FR)	Y

French Guiana	French Franc	N
Gabon	CFA Franc	Y
Gambia	Dalasi (GAD)	Y
Germany*	Deutsche Mark (DMK)	N
Ghana	Cedi (GHC)	Y
Greece	Drachma (DRA)	Y
Guatemala	Quetzal (QUE)	N
Guinea	Franc (GNF)	Y
Guyana	Dollar (GYD)	Y
Honduras	Lempira (LEM)	Y
Hong Kong	Dollar (HKD)	N
Hungary	Forint (FOR)	Y
Iceland	Krona (IKR)	Y
India	Rupee (INR)	Y
Indonesia	Rupiah (RP)	Y
Iran	Rial (IRI)	Y
Iraq	Dinar (IRD)	Y
Ireland*	Punt (IRL)	Y
Israel	Shekel (ILS)	Y
Italy*	Lira (LIT)	N
Jamaica	Dollar (JAD)	Y
Japan	Yen (JYE)	N
Jordan	Dinar (JOD)	Y
Kenya	Shilling (KES)	Y
Korea (South)	Won (WON)	Y
Kuwait	Dinar (KUD)	N
Laos	Kip (KIP)	N
Lebanon	Pound (LEL)	N
Libya	Dinar (LBD)	Y
Luxembourg*	Franc (LFR)	N
Malaysia	Ringgit (RGT)	N
Mali	Franc (CFA)	Y
Malta	Lira (MAL)	Y

Mauritius	Rupee (MAR)	Y
Mexico	Peso (MEP)	N
Micronesia	US Dollar	N
Mongolia	Tugrik	Y
Morocco	Dirham (MDH)	Y
Mozambique	Metical (MZM)	Y
Nepal	Rupee (NER)	Y
Netherlands*	Guilder (DFL)	N
New Zealand	Dollar (NZD)	N
Nicaragua	Cordoba (COR)	N
Nigeria	Naira (NGN)	Y
Norway	Krone (NOK)	Y
Oman	Rials (RIO)	N
Pakistan	Rupee (PAR)	Y
Papua	New Guinea Kina (NGK)	Y
Paraguay	Gurani (GUA)	N
Peru	Inti (PEI)	N
Philippines	Peso (PHP)	Y
Poland	Zloty (ZLO)	N
Portugal*	Escudo (ESP)	Y
Qata	Ryal (QRI)	N
Réunion	French Franc	N
Romania	Lei (LEI)	Y
Russia	Rouble (ROU)	Y
St. Lucia	East Caribbean Dollar	N
Saudi Arabia	Ryal (ARI)	N
Senegal	CFA Franc	Y
Seychelles	Rupee (SER)	N
Sierra Leone	Leone (SLE)	Y
Singapore	Dollar (S$)	N
Solomon Islands	Dollar (SBD)	Y
Somalia	Shilling (SOM)	Y
South Africa	Rand (SAR)	Y

Spain*	Peseta (PTS)	N
Sri Lanka	Rupee (SLR)	Y
Sudan	Pound (SUL)	Y
Sweden	Krona (SEK)	N
Taiwan	Dollar (NTD)	Y
Thailand	Baht (BHT)	Y
Tonga	Pa'anga (T$)	N
Trinidad & Tobago	Dollar (TTD)	Y
Tunisia	Dinar (TUD)	Y
Turkey	Lira (TUL)	Y
Turks & Caicos	U.S. Dollar (US$)	N
Uganda	Shilling (UGS)	Y
U.A.E.	Dirham (ADH)	N
U.K.	Pound (GBP)	N
U.S.A.	Dollar (US$)	N
Uruguay	Peso (NUP)	N
Venezuela	Bolivar (VBO)	N
Vietnam	New Dong (ND)	Y
Yemen	Dinar	Y
Zaire (Dem. Rep. of the Congo)	Zaire (ZAI)	Y
Zambia	Kwacha (ZMK)	Y
Zimbabwe	Dollar (ZWD)	Y

KEY TO CHART

Y   *Yes, currency movements are restricted.*

N   *No, currency movements are not restricted.*

*   *These countries have announced that they will introduce Euro coins and notes in 2002.*

MONEY IN AN EMERGENCY

It is a good idea to keep some of your emergency funds in a bank account at home and ask your bank to grant a mandate to a trusted friend or relative, allowing that person to draw on the account. Then if you do need your cash in an emergency, a telegraphic transfer will usually get this money to you within 24 hours.

Credit Cards. Even if you do not normally use a credit card, it is wise to apply for one before you leave home and take it along with you. In an emergency, you can use it to pay for accommodation, medical bills or your journey home, and settle the bill later. On top of all this, some credit cards give you a limited amount of travel and personal accident insurance cover, besides providing a 24-hour emergency assistance service which you can call for advice should you need it. All this comes free so it is worth looking into.

Discount Cards. A number of cards are available which entitle the holder to a discount on goods and services—including food and drink, accommodation, travel, entertainment and sightseeing—in many countries. These range from 10% off some coach journeys in Australia to 50% off certain air fares in Turkey.

If you are a student, be sure to take along your identification card issued by your school, college or university. It is always worth producing it when you go into a shop, travel agency or hotel as student discounts are often available—but only if you ask!

Also, several international 'identity cards' are available which grant discounts to students and non-students in various countries. These charge a small fee but also come with a directory of organisations which grant discounts to the card holder. Here are two of the main card organisations:

- ISIC (International Student Identity Card). This is available to students from their students' union or from

  ISIC, Bleaklow House, Mill Street
  Glossop, Derbyshire, SK13 8PT, U.K.

- YIDC (International Youth ID Card). This is available to anyone below 26, and not just students, and offers more than 11,000 discount goods and services worldwide. It is available from

FIYTO, 81 Islands Brygge, 2300 Copenhagen S
Denmark.

The cards are also available from several youth agencies
worldwide including:

London Student Travel, 52 Grosvenor Gardens
London, SW1W 0AG
U.K.

and

CIEE, 205 East 42nd Street, New York, NY10017
U.S.A.

PACKING—WHAT TO TAKE AND WHAT TO LEAVE AT HOME

If you are going on a long journey, the best advice is to travel light because you will have to carry all that you take with you. There is no point trying to take everything. It makes better sense to pack only what you need for the first couple of weeks, then buy as you go along.

Sure, you will spend a fortune if you try to buy your usual branded goods in every corner of the globe. Instead, wear what the locals wear as you will find that it is usually cheaper and more suited to the local climate. Here are packing tips that will help:

- A backpack is a more efficient way of carrying your luggage than a suitcase, even if you do not plan on hiking.
- Take along a smaller day bag or backpack so you do not need to carry all your belongings around. If you are job-hunting, lugging a huge backpack does nothing for your image.
- Think ahead about the climate in the places that you will be visiting. The temperature and humidity can vary greatly with latitude, longitude and altitude, and the seasons are reversed in the northern and southern hemispheres.

- Do not take lots of thick clothing, even if you plan to visit a cold country somewhere along your journey. Wearing several layers can keep you just as warm and you can adapt to the temperature by adding or removing those extra layers.
- Take at least one set of smart clothes for interviews or work if you land a job in an office, restaurant or hotel.
- Allow yourself at least one personal luxury—for example, book, diary or personal hi-fi and tapes. It is also worth taking a few other 'luxury' items such as cheap watches, packets of cigarettes, sweets, pens, cosmetics or toiletries when visiting the poorer countries. These can be used as currency or gifts to people who are in a position to help you.
- Do not take anything of any monetary or sentimental value—for example, jewellery or expensive cameras. In many countries, tourists and travellers are a prime target for thieves. A fairly cheap but reliable camera will do just as well.
- If you know where you will be later on in your journey, have your personal possessions sent ahead by parcel post. This is much cheaper than paying for excess baggage on an airline, and you will not have to carry your goods either.

PASSPORTS, VISAS AND PERMITS

Check your passport. Make it a point to apply for it well in advance. If you already have a passport, check its expiry date. Many countries insist that your passport remains valid until three or six months after your departure. If you are going on a long trip, do renew it early.

If your passport is running short of pages for visas, think about renewing it as well. There are a few countries that will not admit you if you do not have a full page left for their visa stamp.

Where Have You Been Before? Some countries do not recognise each other diplomatically and may refuse to admit travellers who have visited those other countries. Any stamps in your passport showing visits to Israel, North Cyprus and Taiwan, for example, can

cause problems at the border. If this is likely to happen, ask your local passport office for help. They may be able to issue you with a duplicate passport.

Will You Need a Visa? Generally, it is best to assume that you do require a visa to visit any other foreign country. There are many exceptions nowadays in which some countries have agreements with others to waive the need for a visa, but do check. If you are a citizen of an EU country, you do not need a visa to visit any other EU country.

The situation also varies depending on what you will be doing in the country concerned. In many cases, you do not need a visa if you are just a tourist but you will have to get one if you plan to work.

How to Get a Visa. Some countries issue visas when you enter at their border. However, many others only issue visas from an embassy or consulate in another country. Again, you must check before leaving home. It will be too late when you are waiting at the border and find that visas are only issued at consulates. If you know you will need a visa to visit a certain country, apply for it before you leave home even if that country is the third or fourth stop on your itinerary.

ENTRY AND RESIDENCE REGULATIONS

Most countries make a distinction between foreigners who stay as tourists and those who wish to work. Most countries welcome tourists who are spending money, but discourage working travellers because they may be taking jobs from the locals.

If You are Travelling as a Tourist. Most countries allow you to stay for a fixed period, assuming you have been issued with any visa that is required. Usually, there is no need to get a permit on arrival but some places expect you to register with the local police. A tourist visit is always limited and this varies locally. The period is usually for about three to six months.

If You are Travelling and Want to Find Work. Most countries expect you to have a work permit. However, they will not usually issue you with a work permit unless you have already found a job and, even then, the chances of it being granted vary greatly. So you will need to find a job first and then apply for a permit. A few countries make this difficult by accepting applications for work permits from outside their country only. Citizens from EU countries wishing to work in another EU country do not need a work permit.

Are You Properly Dressed? When entering most countries, remember that the person manning the immigration desk often has total discretion as to whether to admit you and for how long, even if you have a visa. You can avoid this problem by making sure your passport, visa and any permits are in order and that you have the minimum funds required. Some countries impose dress regulations, so try to dress presentably before arriving at the border.

In a few places, Immigration and Customs officials expect a bribe of cash or a small gift in order to oil the wheels of officialdom. Be prepared if you face such a situation.

Illegal Work. It is important to follow the visa, work and permit regulations of any country you wish to visit. However, it must be said that some working travellers ignore the regulations. It is quite common for travellers to enter a country as tourists and then take on a job. Attitudes towards illegal work vary. Some countries turn a blind eye, but others are strict and offenders can be deported, fined or even jailed.

SAFETY AND SECURITY

Travelling the world can be risky. Some countries have a very high standard of public order with very little crime, whereas others are quite dangerous and the law counts for very little. Most countries fall somewhere in the middle but the difficulty is finding out how safe or risky a country is when you first arrive.

The best advice is to be cautious when you arrive in a new place until you have the chance to size up the local situation. The following tips will help:

- If you can afford it, pay a little more for a hotel with better security, rather than a cheaper one without any.
- Take your own portable door lock for hotel and hostel rooms, plus a padlock and chain to secure your backpack in hostels or on trains.
- At night, take a taxi rather than a bus, and do not walk around town until you determine that it is safe to do so.

TRIGG

- Ask a trusted person such as a tour guide or hotel receptionist where it is safe and not safe to go.
- Do not go out of town at night, unless you know it is safe to do so.
- Keep cash and valuables in a money belt.
- Do not show off your money, jewellery or watch. If you have a camera with you, make sure it is not an expensive one.
- Do not accept offers of accommodation, tours or money-changing from people who come up to you in the street.
- Be wary about accepting food or drink from strangers. It may be genuine hospitality but thieves sometimes use food and drink to drug their victims and make off with their cash and valuables.
- Be wary about accepting job offers as hostesses or dancers in bars and clubs. The jobs may be a front for prostitution.
- When travelling, never carry any packages for people you do not know, even if they offer to pay well. You may unwittingly be helping to smuggle drugs.

CHECKLIST OF USEFUL ITEMS

You will not be able to carry all these items, especially if you are back-packing. However, the list might help to jog your memory when you are packing, just in case you have left out something important.

Documents
- Passport
- Spare passport photos
- Visas
- Insurance certificate
- Foreign currency
- Traveller's cheques
- ID cards
- Discount cards
- Air tickets
- Rail tickets

- Ferry tickets
- Car-hire vouchers
- Hotel addresses
- Hotel accommodation vouchers
- Youth hostel membership cards
- Cards/vouchers
- Maps
- International Driving Permit
- Employers' addresses
- A copy of this book

Vaccinations
- Cholera
- Typhoid
- Polio
- Tetanus
- Yellow fever
- Hepatitis A
- Vaccination certificates

Medical Kit
- Antibiotics
- Anti-malaria tablets
- Anti-diarrhoea treatments
- Any existing medications
- Antiseptic cream
- Antihistamines
- Pain-killers
- Water purification tablets
- Band-aid plasters
- Bandages
- Sterile medical kit
- Eye drops

Toiletries
- Toothpaste
- Soap
- Shampoo
- Razor
- Sanitary protection
- Sun block
- Lip salve
- Condoms
- Toilet paper

Luggage
- Suitcase
- Backpack
- Day bag or backpack

For Campers
- Tent
- Camping stove
- Lamp
- Sleeping bag
- Cooking utensils
- Water bottles

For Skiers
- Salopettes
- Anorak
- Boots
- Skis and poles
- Photos for lift pass

For Photographers
- Camera
- Lenses
- Spare film
- Addresses for developing/printing

Clothing
- Day outfit
- Night/special occasion outfit
- Working clothes—for example, overalls or shirt and tie for bar or hotel jobs
- Thin cotton clothing (warm destinations)
- Thick clothing, or multi-layered items (cold destinations)
- Waterproof items
- Extra underwear (hot and wet destinations)
- Thermal underwear (cold destinations)
- Extra socks (especially for wet or cold destinations)
- Walking shoes/boots
- Day-wear shoes
- Sun hat or cap (sunny/hot destinations)
- Swimming gear
- Sports gear
- Gloves, hat and scarf (cold destinations)

Other Useful Items
- Alarm clock
- Phrase books
- Sunglasses
- Reading material
- Note pad and pens
- Airmail paper and envelopes
- Personal stereo and cassettes
- Binoculars

- Clothes washing kit
- Sewing kit
- Torch and batteries
- Penknife
- Knife, fork and spoon
- Water filter
- Mosquito net
- Matches
- Money belt
- Padlock and chain/portable hotel door lock
- Compass
- Electrical adaptor
- Small gift items (good for making friends)

Chapter Four

OPPORTUNITIES FOR CUT-PRICE TRAVEL

Finding the right way of travelling can be the key to a successful trip. International travel is a strange business. Often, the cost of the journey bears little relationship to the distance and flying from the U.S.A. to Europe, for example, can cost you from as little as US$250 to as much as US$2,000 for the same seat, depending on when and where you buy your ticket.

The well-informed traveller can save much money by planning ahead. This section shows you how to get your travel at bargain-basement prices and, sometimes, even free!

SAVING MONEY ON ROAD TRAVEL

Travelling by road is slow compared to flying and, kilometre for kilometre, is often more expensive taking into account your board, lodging and other expenses along the way. However, it does allow you to see more of the country you are travelling through and really experience its culture.

Hitchhiking. This is the best way of travelling free but it does not work in all countries. In some, drivers go out of their way to pick you up; in others, hitchhiking is almost unknown or even illegal. In many countries, it is not legal to hitch a ride while standing on a public road, so wait for cars emerging from car parks and service stations instead.

If you are hitchhiking, try to look clean and smart, but not too well off! Stand in places where you are visible and where drivers can stop safely. Carrying a destination card will also help. Women should think twice about hitchhiking alone and everyone should avoid it at night. The popularity of hitchhiking has led to the formation of hitchhiking clubs in some countries. Where they exist, these are often listed in the telephone book or Yellow Pages. Some of those in Europe are:

- Germany: Mitfahrzentralen, tel. 089 594561.
- France: Allostop, tel. 12 46 00 66.
- Belgium: Taxistop, tel. 02 511 6930.
- Australia: Travelmates, tel. 09 328 6685 (car-sharing).

Most of these clubs will help you arrange a lift if you give them a few days' notice. They charge a small fee.

Delivering Cars. In some places, it is possible to get free travel by delivering cars over long distances. This is quite common in the U.S.A. where the practice is known as a 'driveaway'. All you pay for is the petrol.

To get this type of work, look in the local newspapers or the telephone directory. You will need a full driving licence. Be wary, though, about driving cars across national borders in case you unintentionally become involved in smuggling.

Courier Work. One way of getting free coach travel is to obtain work as a courier on long-distance coach services. The work involves serving drinks and looking after passengers. To get a job, you should be respectable in appearance and, at least, appear trustworthy. Women stand a better chance. Contact the coach companies for advice.

Driving Jobs. Another way of travelling free by road is to get a driving job, whether travelling by car or lorry. If you have (or plan to get) a driving licence, take it with you. You can also get an International Driving Permit from a motoring organisation in your own country; it will make your licence acceptable in most countries.

To get driving jobs, look into the newspapers or use an employment agency. The Manpower agency has offices in several countries.

Buying a Car. Buying a car to drive to your destination, then selling it when you arrive, can be more practical than you think. It can work out cheaper than the cost of a long air or rail trip, especially if a few of you are travelling together.

Most countries will allow you to enter with a car, as a tourist, without paying Customs duties. However, some countries note this on your passport and will expect you to take the car with you when you leave.

Other Ways of Getting Cheap or Free Road Travel

- Advertise under the 'Lift Wanted' classifieds in the local newspaper, or on local notice boards. There may be someone going your way who will give you a lift free, or if you pay towards petrol costs.
- Plan ahead. A single, long journey is cheaper than several short trips.
- In many countries, booking at travel agencies and tourist offices costs more. Book at the bus station instead.
- Return tickets are often cheaper, per journey, than a one-way ticket. If you do not use the return part of the ticket, you may be able to sell it to someone else.

- Do not pay the fare demanded before asking yourself if there is a cheaper alternative. There usually is, but often, you will find it only if you ask.
- Avoid express services unless you are in a hurry. Such services cost more.
- In the poorer countries, there is often a choice between new, air-conditioned coaches and old, battered ones. You can save a small fortune by giving up a little comfort.

SAVING MONEY ON RAIL TRAVEL

It is virtually impossible to get free rail trips legally. In some places, ticket inspectors are easy-going on foreign travellers who claim to have lost their ticket but in many other countries, heavy fines are imposed. A better way of travelling cheaply is to make sure you travel at the right time (during off-peak seasons, for example), buy the right type of ticket and get it from the right place (which offers a lower price).

Discount Rail Passes. Most national railway companies offer a discount pass for foreign travellers which you can buy before you leave home. Always enquire about discount passes before you leave home but compare the rail fares in your destination to make sure that the pass offers a genuine saving. Unless you intend to do all your travelling by rail, it may not offer you any saving at all.

The Inter-Rail ticket available for one month's unlimited rail travel throughout Europe and Turkey is one of the world's great travel bargains, but only if you are going to do all your travelling by rail. The ticket is available to people of any age (but it is cheaper if you are below 26). It can be bought at most stations and travel agents within Europe.

If you are only going to make a couple of train trips within Europe, a Eurotrain ticket will work out cheaper. Here are more tips on rail travel:

- Some railway companies charge much more for individual tickets booked from foreign countries. Find out before you leave and pre-book only if it does not cost more.

- In some places tourists are charged special inflated 'tourist fares'. Ask a local to buy your ticket and you will find yourself paying less.
- Ask for the right class. Foreigners are often assumed to want to travel first class and will be sold tickets in that class. Ask for second or third class instead.
- Travelling during peak commuter hours can cost double that during off-peak hours, and using a fast express service can cost four times that of a local train that makes scheduled stops. So always shop around for your mode of transport.
- Sleeping compartments are expensive. Take a seat instead and spend the saving on a hotel room when you arrive.
- Offer to buy unused return tickets from passengers arriving at stations who have changed their travel plans.

SAVING MONEY ON SEA TRAVEL

Because there are now fewer ships at sea than in the past (but they are much larger), the opportunities for travelling by sea are not that great. Free lifts and opportunities to work on a passage are rare and paying for a ticket to travel by freighter can be more costly than flying.

Ships' captains will very occasionally take hitchhikers, although company regulations and insurance problems usually forbid it. If you are stuck, it can be worth asking. Ask at the harbour master's office in any port for details of ships and destinations, then see if you can make contact with the captain.

So far as ferries go, lorry drivers will sometimes let hitchhikers travel with them, as will car drivers, as the fare usually covers the vehicle and an unlimited number of passengers. All you can do is travel to the port and go from vehicle to vehicle, hoping someone will take you.

Working on a Cruise Ship. If you can find this type of work, you will not only travel free, but get paid for it as well. The cruise business is expanding rapidly and thousands of jobs are available every year. To get a job on a cruise ship, you will need to have experience in a corresponding land-based job such as waiting on tables, kitchen work, hairdressing, bar work, entertaining or sports instruction.

More information about getting work on cruise ships is given in Chapter Two of this book. Most of these vacancies are handled by the shipping companies or employment agencies on land, although you can turn up when a likely-looking cruise ship comes into port and ask if there are any vacancies.

Yachts. There are now thousands of yachts at sea and there is a need for casual staff. Indeed, some of the yachts owned by the world's richest people are luxurious and require up to 20 or 30 crew members. Usually, no skills are required although skills in cooking, cleaning and maintenance will prove useful. Some sailing experience will also help you get the job more easily.

To get this kind of work, just show up at ports and harbours or, if you want to arrange a trip in advance, get in touch with a crewing agency. These are found in most port towns and cities where yachts gather. Crewitt in the U.K. can be contacted on 01202 678847.

Travelling on a Cargo Ship. At one time, cargo vessels regularly took passengers, and at bargain-priced fares. Nowadays, however, most cargo vessels do not take passengers and even if they do, the fares are not cheap. If, however, you fancy this form of travel, the *ABC Passenger Shipping Guide* gives details of all cargo routes which carry passengers. If you have difficulty finding a copy, contact the publishers in the U.K. on 01582 600111.

Working a Passage. Modern ships are largely mechanised and do not have much need for unskilled hands. That said, a few adventurous travellers manage to find work all the same. If you are interested, try writing to shipping companies (listed in the *Register of Shipping* published by Lloyd's Register). Or you can turn up at the port and ask ships' captains, harbour masters or cargo agents.

You will stand a better chance of getting a job if you have relevant experience, such as painting, cooking and joinery or electrical skills, and also if you have been to sea before, even if you have only crewed a yacht.

Fishing Boats. Fishing boats and similar vessels such as inshore coasters and ferries offer a better chance of a free trip than the large container vessels or tankers—firstly, because there are many more of them and secondly, because their captains are more likely to be approachable. There is no easy way you can line these trips up other than making the journey down to the nearest port. The offer of a small payment (or cigarettes, alcohol, etc.) may be enough to get you a trip.

Other Methods. Do not be tempted to travel as a stowaway on a ship. There have been cases where stowaways have been thrown into the sea!

SAVING MONEY ON AIR TRAVEL

Believe it or not, air travel is usually cheaper, kilometre for kilometre, than any other form of travel. It is also one of the few forms of travel where it is virtually impossible to travel free, so concentrate on getting your ticket in the cheapest way possible. If you know how to buy your ticket, it is possible to travel by air for less than what it costs the airline to provide you with the seat!

Escort Travel. A few jobs are available which involve escorting children, the sick, the elderly or disabled persons on long-distance journeys by air. However, there are not many opportunities and if you are interested, you should call up the various airlines in your area. Some kind of nursing or childcare experience is desirable.

Air Courier Travel. An air courier gets a free or low-cost return flight to a destination in return for travelling with important packages. To get this kind of trip, you will have to register with an air courier company at least 14 days in advance, stating your destination. You can find your local air courier company in the Yellow Pages. Your trip, however, is subject to availability.

If travelling free or cheaply as a courier, you will not be allowed to take anything more than hand baggage since your luggage allowance is taken up by the packages, which are usually important business documents, medical supplies, machine parts and so on.

One strict rule applies to such work. Always make sure you go to a reputable and well-established courier company. Do not take up offers of courier work from people you do not know as you may find yourself involved in drug smuggling. If a company or individual offers to pay you to work as a courier, it is a sign that something is not right as reputable courier firms do not need to pay people to work for them.

More tips for saving money on your air ticket

- Never telephone an airline and book a seat. The prices are really for business travellers.
- If you use the services of a travel agent, always ask if there is a cheaper flight. You can often get one if you modify your plans and fly on a different airline, on a different day or at a different time.
- Use youth and student travel agencies if possible, since airlines often have special deals on offer. There is STA Travel in London (0171 937 9962) and New York (1 800 925 4777).

- Join a discount travel club such as WEXAS at 45-49 Brompton Road, Knightsbridge, London, SW3 IDE, U.K., tel. 0171 589 3315.
- Unusual routes which involve stopovers and connecting flights can be much cheaper than non-stop journeys. Examine all the options. For example, flying from the U.K. to the U.S.A. with a stop in Amsterdam may be a little inconvenient, but will usually be cheaper than a direct flight.
- Book with lesser-known airlines. They are usually cheaper than nationally owned airlines. As long as the airline is an IATA member (this will be marked on the ticket), your money is protected.
- The less restricted your ticket is, the more expensive it will be. In other words, if you buy a ticket for a definite flight which cannot be cancelled, rather than an open ticket, you will almost always save money.

OTHER WAYS OF TRAVELLING CHEAP OR FREE

Unusual opportunities may come your way but the tried and tested route includes the following.

Package Holidays. A package holiday offering a return flight and accommodation often works out cheaper than the cost of the full-fare flight alone. Simply use the outward ticket for travel but do not use the accommodation or return travel if you do not want it.

Cycling. Many countries are ideal for cycling—for example, Holland, Germany, France and even China. If you do not want to take a bicycle along, you can buy or rent one along the way.

Safaris. Several companies are now offering overland safaris through Europe, trans-Africa, or into South America. If you have some mechanical knowledge, you may apply to be taken along free as a spare mechanic and/or driver. Ring up some of the companies to enquire. (There are some addresses in the 'Africa' section of the directory listing in the next chapter.)

Removal Services. Long-distance removal companies need labourers to pack the truck, travel with a load and then unpack it at the other end. You may have to work a day or two without pay at either end but can expect to travel free and be entitled to free food and accommodation. Try companies in the Yellow Pages.

Chapter Five

COUNTRY-BY-COUNTRY DIRECTORY

In this chapter, you will find most of the countries listed under their own headings, while the smaller ones may be grouped under a broader heading such as 'Asia' or 'The Caribbean'. Listings are in alphabetical order, and telephone numbers are supplied where available.

You may want to read up further about how to cope with living and working in the various countries. The *Culture Shock* series has been written towards this end. The countries covered include Australia, Bolivia, Britain, Canada, Chile, China, Cuba, Czech

Republic, Denmark, Egypt, France, Germany, Greece, Hong Kong, India, Indonesia, Iran, Ireland, Israel, Italy, Japan, Korea, Laos, Malaysia, Mauritius, Morocco, Myanmar, Nepal, Netherlands, Norway, Pakistan, Philippines, Singapore, South Africa, Spain, Sri Lanka, Sweden, Switzerland, Syria, Taiwan, Thailand, Turkey, U.A.E., U.S.A., Ukraine, Venezuela and Vietnam.

Under the Job Leads listing, the following codes are used to identify the types of jobs available:

☘	Agriculture/Farming Jobs
👬	Au Pair/Nannying Jobs
☻	Construction Jobs
⚠	Yacht Crew Members
⊞	Domestic Jobs
✕	Hotel and/or Restaurant Work
👫	Jobs on Summer Camps for Children
⊕	Jobs in Tourism—for example, guides and couriers
✎	Teaching Jobs
♥	Voluntary Work

AFRICA

* See individual headings for information on South Africa and Egypt.

Author's Comment. Africa is not the easiest country to travel through and job opportunities are few and far between. But everyone should try to spend some time in Africa, even if it is just a couple of days in Kenya or the Sudan.

Jobs You Can Do. Opportunities are fairly scarce. Voluntary work with an established agency is a good idea, even if you do not get paid. In some major cities, you may be able to get a job in an office, or teach English. If you have some mechanical knowledge, you can try for a job with a safari company.

What About Daily Life? Very cheap and basic in most places. Take along everything you need and remember that in a lot of places, you cannot take things like good medical care and clean water for granted.

Entry Regulations. Get details from the nearest consulate of the countries you plan to visit as requirements vary a great deal. If you need a visa, make sure you get it before you leave home as border officials in Africa are very strict about who they admit.

Job Leads

ACCAAEJ
Centre Culkturel, Nacira 35250
W. Boumerdes
Algeria. (♥)

Africa Explored
Rose Cottage, Summerleaze
Magor, Newport, Gwent
NP6 3DE, U.K. (◉)

African-American Institute
833 UN Plaza, New York
NY10017, U.S.A. (♥)

Africa Venture
10 Market Place
Devizes, SN10 1HT
U.K. (✎)

African Voluntary Service of Sierra Leone
PMB 717, Freetown
Sierra Leone. (❤)

Association Tunisienne de l'Action Volontaire
Maison du Parti, Boulevard du 9 Avril
La Kasbah, 1002 Tunis
Tunisia. (❤)

BWA
P.O. Box 1185, Mochudi
Botswana. (❤)

CCM/YL
P.O. Box 19985, Dar Es Salaam
Tanzania. (❤)

Chantiers Jeunesse Maroc
GCP Rabat No.1234
P.O. Box 556, Rabat Chellah
Morocco. (❤)

Chantiers Sociaux Marocains
P.O. Box 456, Rabat
Morocco. (❤)

DAPP
Job-os, Box 131, 2630 Taastrup
Denmark.
(Voluntary work projects in Angola.)

Dragoman
Camp Green, Debenham
Suffolk, IP14 6LA
U.K. (⊚)

Frontier
77 Leonard Street, London. EC2 4QS
U.K.
(Environmental voluntary work in Tanzania and Uganda.)

Encounter Overland
267 Old Brompton Road, London, SW5 9JA
U.K. (⊚)

Exodus Expeditions
9 Weir Road, London, SW12 0LT
U.K. (⊚)

Guerba Expeditions
101 Edenvale Road, Westbury, Wiltshire, BA13 3QX
U.K. (⊚)

Kenya Voluntary Development Association
P.O. Box 48902, Nairobi
Kenya. (♥)

Kumuka Africa
42 Westbourne Grove, London, W2
U.K. (⊚)

Nigerian Voluntary Service
P.O. Box 11837, Ibadan
Nigeria. (♥)

Pensee et Chantiers
BP 1423, Rabat
Morocco. (❤)

Student Council of Kenya
Mamlaka Road, P.O. Box 54579, Nairobi
Kenya. (❤)

Tracks
The Flots, Brookland, Romney Marsh
Kent, TN29 9TG
U.K. (🌀)

VOLU
P.O. Box 1540, Accra
Ghana. (❤)

VWAN
P.O. Box 2189, Lagos
Nigeria. (❤)

Zimbabwe Workcamps Association
P.O. Box CY2039, Causeway, Harare
Zimbabwe. (❤)

Help with Travel and Accommodation

Association Tunisienne des Auberges de Jeunesse
10 rue Ali Bach Hamba
BP320-1015 Tuni
Tunisia.

Fédération Algérienne des Auberges de Jeunesse
213 Rue Hassiba Ben Bouali
BP 15, El-Annasser 160115, Algiers
Algeria.

Fédération Royal Marocaine des Auberges de Jeunes
Boulvard Okba Ben Nafii, Meknes
Morocco.
Tel. 05 524698

Kenya Youth Hostels Association
P.O. Box 48661, Nairobi
Kenya
Tel. 723012

Sudanese Youth Hostels Association
P.O. Box 1705, Khartoum
Sudan
Tel. 81464

ASIA
See individual headings for information on China and Japan.

Author's Comment. Every world trip should include at least some time wandering through two or three Asian countries. They are places where old meets new, and where ancient temples stand alongside the most modern buildings. The contrasts and culture shock experienced from country to country can be tremendous. While places like Singapore and Hong Kong are poised at the edge of the 21st century, parts of Vietnam and Myanmar (formerly known as Burma) have barely entered the 20th.

Jobs You Can Do. For native English speakers, the teaching of the language is one of the most popular and acceptable ways of earning a living, especially in Hong Kong, South Korea, Taiwan and Thailand. In most Asian cities, there are also many jobs available in offices, hotels, restaurants and bars but unless you are a national of that country, it may not be easy for you to obtain a work permit to take on the job legally. A few charities operate voluntary work projects, although there is not as much choice as in the poorer Third World countries. There are also opportunities for au pair work in some countries.

What About Daily Life? The Asian cities are big, busy and very modern, with all the facilities you will find in London or New York. But living costs in some of the cities can be quite high. Rural areas in the less developed countries can be very quiet and the lifestyle has changed little over the centuries, so be prepared for a simple way of life. Wages for the teaching of English are fairly modest, so you will need to balance your budget carefully.

Entry Regulations. Check before travelling as the situation varies from country to country.

Job Leads

Drake International
18th Floor, Peregrine Tower, Lippo Centre
Hong Kong. (Office jobs)
Tel. 2523 8781

EMC Staff
The Landmark, 11 Pedder Street, Central
Hong Kong.
(HR, Office jobs)

Frontier
77 Leonard Street, London, EC2 4QS
U.K.
(Environmental voluntary work projects in Vietnam.)

Involvement Volunteers Association
P.O. Box 218, Port Melbourne, VIC3207
Australia. (♥)

Korean National Committee for UNESCO
P.O. Box C64, Seoul
South Korea. (♥)

Neejay Agency
223 Nathan Road, Kowloon
Hong Kong. (HR, office jobs)

NENAK
163 Suriwong Road, Bangkok, Thailand. (✎)

Nightingales
17 Charnwood Grove, West Bridgford, Notts, NG2 7NT
U.K.(👬)
Tel. 0115 982 2338

Owens Personnel
New World Tower, 16-18 Queen's Road Central
Hong Kong. (Office jobs)
Tel. 3845 6220

Search Associates
P.O. Box 168, Chiang Mai, 5000
Thailand. (✎)

Stable Relief Service
The Old Rectory, Belton in Rutland, Uppingham
Leicestershire, LE15 9LE
U.K. (👫, ♨)
Tel. 01572 86381

Staff Service
15th Floor Shell Tower
Time Square, Hong Kong
Tel. 2506 2676 (Business/Commercial)

Taiwan Cultural Institute
44 Davies Street, London, W1Y 2BL
U.K. (✎)

United Nations Association Wales
International Youth Service, Temple of Peace, Cathays Park
Cardiff, CF1 3AP
U.K. (❤)
Tel. 01222 223088

Voluntary Service Overseas (VSO)
317 Putney Bridge Road, London, SW15 2PN
U.K. (❤)

Newspapers
(To check job vacancies in the classifieds.)

South China Morning Post (Hong Kong)
South China Post (Taiwan)
Bangkok Post (Thailand)

Help with Travel and Accommodation

Chinese Taipei Youth Hostel Association
12F-14, 50 Chung Hsiao West Road Section 1, Taipei
Taiwan.
Tel. 331 8366

Hong Kong Youth Hostels Association
Room 225, Block 19, Shek Kip Mei Estate, Shamshuio, Kowloon
Hong Kong.
Tel. 852 788 1638

Indonesian Youth Hostels Association
Graha Pemuda Lantai 8, Jalan Gerbang Pemuda 3
Senayan, Jakarta 10270
Indonesia.
Tel. 588156

Korea Youth Hostels Association
604 Seoul Youth Centre, 27 Soopyo-Dong
Joong-ku, Seoul
South Korea.
Tel. 02 266 2896

Malaysian Youth Hostels Association
21 Jalan Kampung Attap, 50460 Kuala Lumpur
Malaysia.
Tel. 03 230 6870

Thai Youth Hostels Association
25/2 Phitsanulok Road, Sisao Theves
Dusit, Bangkok 10300
Thailand.
Tel. 282 0950

AUSTRALIA

Author's Comment. Friendly people, good weather and great sight-seeing make Australia a must for any world traveller. Sydney offers many job opportunities and an interesting social life, but it is also worth spending some time in the virtually uninhabited bush, plus some time in Queensland's fun-filled Gold Coast resorts.

Jobs You Can Do. Almost anything. Jobs in shops, hotels, restaurants, bars and offices, as well as fruit-picking, are favourites with working travellers.

What About Daily Life? Food and accommodation are reasonably inexpensive but if you are touring, do not underestimate the cost as the popular places may be far-flung and distances are great.

Entry Regulations. Visitors from most countries except New Zealand require a visa, obtainable in advance from any Australian Consulate. Young people from some countries (including the U.K., Ireland, Canada, Netherlands and Japan) who are between the ages of 18 and 25 can obtain a special Working Holiday Visa which entitles them to apply for any job in Australia. However, they are not allowed to accept any job offer until they arrive in Australia, although there is nothing to stop them from making enquiries before they leave. The Working Holiday Visa covers a maximum of 12 months.

Job Leads

Au Pair Australia
6 Wilford Street, Corrimal, NSW 2519
Australia. (👪)

Australian Trust for Conservation Volunteers
P.O. Box 423, Ballarat, Victoria 3350
Australia. (❤, ♨)

93

British Universities North America Club (BUNAC)
16 Bowling Green Lane, London, EC1R 0BD, U.K.
Tel. 0171 251 3472
(Various jobs available to U.K. students only.)

International Agricultural Exchange Association
Stoneleigh Park, Kenilworth
Warwickshire CV8 2LG,
U.K. (⚑)

Involvement Volunteers Association
P.O. Box 218, Port Melbourne, Victoria 3207
Australia. (❤)

Northern Victoria Fruit Growers Association
P.O. Box 394, Shepparton, Victoria 3630
Australia. (⚑)

Stablemate
156 Pitt Town Road
Kenthurst 2156, Australia
(Work with horses worldwide.)

Victoria Peach and Apricot Growers Association
P.O. Box 39, Cobram, Victoria 3644
Australia. (⚑)

Visitoz
1a Benbow Road
Hammersmith, London W6 0AT, U.K.
(Various kinds of work in Australia.)

Willing Workers on Organic Farms
W. Tree, Buchan, Victoria 3885
Australia. (⚑)

Job Agencies

National Employment Services (known as the CES)

45 Grenfell Street, Adelaide.
215 Adelaide Street, Brisbane.
128 Bourke Street, Melbourne.
186 St. George's Terrace, Perth.
818-820 George Street, Sydney.

Private Employment Agencies in Australia

All Catering Staff
2 Grosvenor Street, Bondi Junction
Sydney.
Tel. 02 389 0155

Drake Personnel
9 Queen Street, Melbourne.
60 Margaret Street, Sydney.
Tel. 02 241 4488
10 Moore Street, Canberra.

ECCO
18 Bent Street
Melbourne.

Manpower
34 Hunter Street, Sydney.
Tel. 02 231 4844
307 Queens Street, Brisbane

Temporary Solutions
275 George Street
Sydney.
Tel. 02 201 3677

World Traveller's Network
3 Orwell Street
Sydney.
Tel. 02 357 4425
(Offers help and advice to those holding
Working Holiday Visas.)

Newspapers

Sydney Morning Herald (Sydney)
Courier & Mail (Brisbane)
The West Australian (Adelaide)
The Melbourne Age (Melbourne)

Help with Travel and Accommodation

Australian Youth Hostels Association
Level 3, 10 Mallett Street
Camperdown, NSW2050
Australia.
Tel. 02 565 1699

Backpacker's Resorts
P.O. Box 1000, Byron Bay, NSW2481
Australia.
(Operates 120 hostels around Australia.)

YHA Travel
176 Day Street, Sydney. NSW2000
Australia.
Tel. 02 267 3044
(YHA members qualify for 10% discount on coach travel, car hire,
tours and other goods and services.)

AUSTRIA

Author's Comment. Austria is a clean, well-organised country and, being small, has limited potential for working travellers. The winter ski resorts offer the greatest number of job opportunities.

Jobs You Can Do. Hotel, bar and restaurant work is popular. Au-pairing is popular in Vienna.

What About Daily Life? Austria is quite an expensive country to live in and it is difficult to get by on a tight budget. Accommodation and social life will cut into your budget so take enough money with you. Wages are good but employers are demanding and may expect you to work long hours.

Entry Regulations. A visa is required by most nationalities and must be obtained from an Austrian Consulate before arriving in Austria. Citizens of other EU countries do not need a visa or work permit.

Job Leads

Academy Au Pair & Nanny Agency Ltd
42 Cedarhurst Drive, London, SE9 5LP
U.K.
Tel. 0181 294 1191 (👬)

Arbeitsgemeinschaft Auskandssozialdienst Katholisches
Jugenwerk Osterreichs
Johannesgasse 16/1, 1010 Vienna
Austria. (👫)

Canvas Holidays
12 Abbey Park Place, Dunfermline, Fife, KY12 7PD
U.K. (🐚)

Crystal Holidays
The Courtyard, Arlington Road, Surbiton, KT6 6BW
U.K. (🐚)
Tel. 0181 241 5111

OKISTA
Garnisongasse 7, 1090 Vienna,
Austria. (👫)

Osterreichischer Bauorden
P.O. Box 186, Hornegasse, 1031 Vienna
Austria. (❤)

SCI
Schottengasse 3A, 1010 Vienna,
Austria. (❤)

Ski Total
10 Hill Street, Richmond. Surrey, TW9 0LT
U.K.
Tel. 0181 948 3535 (🐚, 🏠)

Young Austria
Alpenstrasse 108a, 5020 Salzburg
Austria. (👫)

Job Agencies

National Employment Services

Bebenbergerstrasse 33, A-8021 Graz.
Schopfstrasse 5, Innsbruck.
Schiesstantstrasse 4, A-5021 Salzburg.
Hohenstauffengasse 2, A-1013 Vienna.
Weihburggasse 30, Vienna.

Newspapers

Die Press
Der Standard
Wiener Zeitung
Neue Tiroler Zeitung
Tiroler Tageszeitung
Salzburger Volkszeitung

Help with Travel and Accommodation

Austrian Foreign Students Service
Rooseveltplatz 13, 1090 Vienna
Austria.

OKISTA
Garnisongasse 7, 1090 Vienna
Austria.
(Can help you find a place to live.)

BELGIUM

Author's Comment. Belgium is at the heart of Europe and very international in its outlook. You will meet people from all over Europe living and working in Brussels.

Jobs You Can Do. Hotel, bar and restaurant work is popular, as is community or voluntary work. If you are staying for some time, you can get a job in an office.

What About Daily Life? Belgium is a multilingual society speaking Flemish in the north and French in the south. Both are spoken in Brussels, but it is easier to find a job there if you speak some French.

Entry Regulations. Citizens of EU countries do not need a visa or work permit. Citizens of other countries need a visa so check with your nearest Belgian Consulate before leaving.

Job Leads

ATD Quart Monde
Avenue Victor Jacobs 12, 1040 Brussels
Belgium. (♥)

Avalon Au Pairs
Thursely House, 53 Station Road, Shalford
Guildford, Surrey, GU4 8HA
U.K. (👫)
Tel. 01483 63640

Carrefour Chantiers
25 Boulevard de l'Empereur, 1000 Brussels
Belgium. (♥)

Contiki Holidays
Wells House, 15 Elmfield Road, Bromley, Kent, BR1 1LS
U.K. (◉)

Eurocamp Plc
Knutsford, Cheshire WA16 0NL
U.K. (◉)

MJP
Boulevard de l'Empereur 15, 1000 Brussels
Belgium. (♥)

SCI
Rue Van Elewyck 35, 1050 Brussels
Belgium. (♥)

The Au Pair Agency
231 Hale Lane, Edgware, Middlesex, HA8 9QF
U.K. (👫)
Tel. 0181 958 1750

Via
Venusstraat 28, 2000 Antwerp
Belgium. (♥)

Job Agencies

National Employment Services

Look for VDAB offices in the Flanders area of Belgium and
ONEM offices in Wallonia. Both will advise on suitable job
vacancies in their own areas.

Head office of VDAB and ONEM
Boulevard de l'Empereur 7
1000 Brussels.

In Brussels, the main ONEM office is at
38 Rue d'Escalier, 1000 Brussels.

Temporary vacancies are dealt with at T-Service bureaux.
The main office in Brussels is at
69 Boulevard Anspach.

Private Employment Agencies

ECCO
17a Rue Vilian XIV, 1050 Brussels.
Tel. 02 647 87 80

Avenue Louise Interim
207 Avenue Louise, 1050 Brussels.
Tel. 02 640 91 91

Select Interim
1-5 Avenue de la Joyeuse Entrée, 1040 Brussels.
Tel. 02 231 03 33

Creyf's
473 Avenue Louise, 1050 Brussels.
Tel. 02 646 34 34

Newspapers

Le Soir
Antwerpse Morgan
La Meusse

In Brussels, you can also refer to *Belgique No. l* (free), *L'Echo* (free) and *The Bulletin* (an English-language newspaper advertising many vacancies for casual jobs).

Help with Travel and Accommodation

CNIJ
10 Rue Jean Volders, 1060 Brussels
Belgium.
(CNIJ will advise on travel, accommodation, jobs and what is happening around town.)

ACOTRA
Rue de la Madeleine 51, 1000 Brussels
Belgium.
(Discounted rates for travel are available.)

BULGARIA

Author's Comment. Bulgaria used to be known as the Eastern-bloc state that was more like Russia than Russia. In recent years, Bulgaria has opened up fast, aiming to make tourism a major export earner. The Black Sea beach resorts boast impressive beaches and the mountains are breathtaking, but do not expect much Western sophistication or luxury.

Jobs You Can Do. It is a choice between teaching English or working in tourism—and even then there are not many jobs available.

What About Daily Life? Inexpensive, but getting costlier. Some of the Black Sea resorts have experienced an increase in crime.

Entry Regulations. A visa is needed if you wish to work, and for tourists who are not travelling as part of a group or on a package tour.

Job Leads

Albena Tourist Company
9620 Albena
Bulgaria. (❌, 🌐)

Argo M
Boulevard Stambolksi 2A, Sofia
Bulgaria. (❤)

Balkan Holidays International
Sofia
Bulgaria. (❌, 🌐)

East European Partnership
317 Putney Bridge Road, London, SW15 2LN
U.K. (❤)

Interbalkan Travel Agency
8 Pozitano Str., 1000 Sofia
Bulgaria. (❌, 🌐)

International Travel Agency
5 Gourko Str., Sofia
Bulgaria. (❌, 🌐)

Las Vegas Casino Hotels
131 Marija Luiza Boulevard, Sofia
Bulgaria. (✖, ◉)

MAR
1387 Sofia
Bulgaria. (❤)

NCVB
11 Stambolski, Sofia 1000
Bulgaria. (❤)

Orbita Tours
76 Anton Avanov Boulevard, 1407 Sofia
Bulgaria. (✖, ◉)

Pamporovo Resort
4870 Pamporovo
Bulgaria. (✖, ◉)

Riviera Holiday Club
Golden Sands
Bulgaria. (✖, ◉)

Shipka Travel Agency
6 Sv. Sofia Str., 1090 Sofia
Bulgaria. (✖, ◉)

Sunny Beach Resort
8240 Slanchev Briag
Bulgaria. (✖, ◉)

Zlatni Piasaci Tourist Company
Varna BG
Bulgaria. (✖, ◉)

Job Agencies

Student Labour Office
P.O. Box 504, Plovdiv 4000
Bulgaria.
Tel. 032 226756
(For students only.)

Help with Travel and Accommodation

Orbita
Boulevard Stamboliski 45, Sofia
Bulgaria

CANADA

Author's Comment. Canada is a vast country with large areas of wilderness. English speakers are most at home in Vancouver. Although thousands of immigrants have been received in the past, the opportunities to stay and work here are quite limited now.

Jobs You Can Do. Voluntary work is the main type of legal work on offer. Jobs in shops, hotels or offices are available to students who can apply for a summer employment visa. Suitable applicants can obtain a visa to work as a care assistant under the Live-in Caregiver Program but there is no au pair programme as such.

What About Daily Life? Canada is relatively inexpensive but travel costs a lot because of the distances involved. Try and spend some time in the wilderness. Outside cities, the lifestyle is fairly unsophisticated.

Entry Regulations. All travellers intending to work need a working visa which is hard to obtain. Students can apply for a special 12-month International Student Summer Employment visa. Ask your nearest Canadian High Commission or Consulate for details of the Live-in Caregiver Program if you are interested in this type of work. You must first find a job from outside Canada, then apply to a Canadian High Commission or Consulate at home for a visa. The number of visas given out is limited.

Job Leads

British Universities North America Club (BUNAC)
16 Bowling Green, London, EC1R OBD
U.K.
Tel. 0171 251 3472
(Various types of work for U.K. students only.)

Canadian Parks Service
Room 200, 10 Wellington Street, Ottawa, K1A OH3
Canada. (♥, ☙)

Canadian Bureau for International Education (CBIE)
85 Albert Street, 14th Floor, Ottawa, K1P 6A4
Canada. (♥)

Christian Movement for Peace
427 Bloor St. West, Toronto, M5S 1XY
Canada. (♥)

Council in International Education Exchange
33 Seymour Place, London, W1H 6AT
U.K.
Tel. 0171 706 3008
(A programme for students only, enabling participants
to apply for any job.)

Environment Canada
Hull, Quebec. K1A 0H3
Canada. (♥)

Frontiers
2615 Danforth Avenue, Toronto. Ontario, M4C 1L6
Canada. (♥)

Langtrain International
Torquay Road, Foxrock, Dublin
Ireland. (👫)
Tel. 1 289 3876

Nannies Unlimited
P.O. Box 5864, Station A, Calgary. Alberta, TZH 1X4
Canada. (👫)

Workers for Organic Farms
2 Carlson Road, Nelson. British Columbia, V1L 5PS
Canada. (♨)

Newspaper

Canada Employment Weekly
24 Noble Street, Suite 303, Toronto, M6K 2C8
Canada.
Tel. 416 536 6461

Help with Travel and Accommodation

The Canadian Bureau for International Education
Suite 1100, 220 Laurier Avenue West,
Ottawa, Ontario, K1P 5Z9
Canada.

THE CARIBBEAN

Author's Comment. The palm-fringed beaches of the Caribbean islands make a dream destination for a working trip. However, jobs are fairly few and far between. Make sure you have a sizeable emergency fund and do not be too sure that you will find any suitable work.

Jobs You Can Do. There are jobs on yachts and cruise ships (mainly with Florida-based ships) and some voluntary projects. You may find a job in a hotel but there are not many opportunities for foreigners.

What About Daily Life? Most of the Caribbean countries are popular luxury tourist resorts, so foreigners will find them expensive to live in. Expenses include travel from island to island and it is not cheap to go island hopping.

Entry Regulations. Check first. Tourists of most nationalities do not need a visa but workers do. The visas are very difficult to obtain.

Job Leads

Atlantic Associates
990 NW 166th Street, Miami, FL33126
U.S.A.
(Recruits staff for cruise ships.)

American Friends Service Committee
1501 Cherry Street, Philadelphia, PA19102
U.S.A. (♥)

Amigos de las Americas
5618 Star Lane, Houston, TX77057.
U.S.A. (♥)

British Universities North America Club (BUNAC)
16 Bowling Green Lane
London, EC1R 0BD
U.K.
Tel. 0171 251 3472
(Various summer opportunities in Jamaica for students only.)

Cruise Line Appointments
Arbour Walk Circle
Suite 2024
Naples. FL34109
U.S.A.
(Opportunities for work on cruise ships.)

Cuba Solidarity Campaign
129 Seven Sisters Road
London, N7 7QC
U.K.
Tel. 0171 263 6452 (❤)

Princess Cruises
10100 Santa Monica Boulevard, Suite 1800
Los Angeles, CA90067-4189
U.S.A.
(Opportunities for work on cruise ships.)

Royal Caribbean Cruises
1050 Caribbean Way
Miami, FL33132-2601
U.S.A.
(Opportunities for work on cruise ships.)

Sea Chest Associates
7385 West Roadway, New Orleans, Louisiana
U.S.A.
(Recruits staff for cruise ships.)

CHINA

Author's Comment. China is a fascinating country offering the Western traveller what is, perhaps, the greatest culture shock anywhere on earth. Travelling independently within China may present some difficulties but any world trip should include at least a week there, even if you only pop over from Hong Kong nearby.

Jobs You Can Do. The only official vacancies available are as a foreign teacher or specialist in some fields of work.

What About Daily Life? This is very cheap and basic. Do not expect a hectic social life but there are many opportunities for sightseeing and meeting the locals, who are very friendly and keen to meet you. You can get most of life's little luxuries in the cities, especially if you have Western currency to spend. Although China is now more 'open' as a country, the political situation is still very sensitive. The political regime does not appreciate criticism and you should respect this situation when living or travelling there.

Entry Regulations. You must have a visa before travelling to China.

Job Leads

To find out more about being a foreign teacher, contact the Chinese Educational Association for International Exchange, 37 Damucang Hutong, Beijing 100816, tel. 1602 0731. Information is also available from your nearest Chinese Embassy, or try the Cultural Section of the Chinese Embassy in the U.K., U.S.A. and Australia at the following addresses:

Birch Grove, London, W3 9SW
U.K.
Tel. 0181 993 0279

2300 Connecticut Avenue NW, Washington DC.
U.S.A.
Tel. 202 328 2563

14 Federal Highway, Watson, Canberra ACT 2602
Australia.
Tel. 241 2446

Many people travelling to China find that they are offered casual work opportunities such as teaching English privately, helping with translations or doing work of a journalistic nature. Such work, however, would be purely on an unofficial basis.

Help with Travel and Accommodation

CYTS Tours Corporation
23B Dong Ziao Min Xiang, Beijing 100006
China
Tel. 861 512770

CZECH REPUBLIC

Author's Comment. Thousands of travellers flock to Prague during summer and if you visit the place, you will know why. It is really one of Europe's finest cities, especially if you are a culture or architecture buff. If you are not, you will be pleased to know that the social life there is very good too.

Jobs You Can Do. The teaching of English is the mainstay for most working travellers. There are a few casual jobs in restaurants and bars and you may be able to line up a job as an au pair. There are many opportunities for voluntary work.

What About Daily Life? Inexpensive. The Czech Republic will not overstretch your budget. Most jobs allow you to get by although they do not pay much by Western standards. Like most eastern European countries nowadays, the Czech Republic is democratic and the government and people are fairly open-minded.

Entry Regulations. EU nationals do not need a visa for a stay of less than a month (as a tourist). Others should check first. If you plan to work, you will need a residence permit from the Czech Embassy at home.

Help with Travel and Accommodation

Czech Youth & Student Travel Bureau (CKM)
Zitna Ulice 12, 12105 Prague
Czech Republic.

Job Leads

Brit-Pol Health Care Foundation
Gerrard House, Worthing Road, East Preston, W. Sussex
U.K. (✎)

Brontosaurus
Kanclear Brontosaura, Bubenska 6, Prague 7
Czech Republic. (❤)

CKM
Zitna Ulice 12, 12105 Prague
Czech Republic. (♥)

Czechpoint GB
56 Wandsworth Road, Hampton, Middlesex, TW12 1ER
U.K. (✎)

East European Partnership
317 Putney Bridge Road, London, SW15 2LN
U.K. (♥)

Inex
Senovazne Namesti 24, 11647 Prague 1
Czech Republic. (♥)

DENMARK

Author's Comment. Denmark is a pleasant, clean country with friendly people, many of whom speak some English. There is not very much to see and do apart from Copenhagen, which buzzes in summer and is a good springboard from which to explore Scandinavia.

Jobs You Can Do. Hotel, restaurant and bar work; also work on farms and in fruit-picking. Plenty of opportunities exist for au pairs.

What About Daily Life? Denmark can be expensive, especially where accommodation is concerned. Although many people speak English, you will get along better if you can learn a little Danish. Culturally, the country has much in common with its northern neighbours Norway, Sweden and Finland which, together with itself, comprise Scandinavia.

Entry Regulations. EU citizens do not need a visa or work permit. Other citizens must apply for a visa if they wish to work, but opportunities for them are limited.

Job Leads

Academy Au Pair & Nanny Agency Ltd
42 Cedarhurst Drive, London, SE9 5LP
U.K.
Tel. 0181 850 8932 (👫)

Avalon Au Pairs
Thursely House, 53 Station Road, Shalford, Guildford, Surrey,
GU4 8HA
U.K. (👫)
Tel. 01483 63640

Eurocamp Plc
Knutsford, Cheshire WA16 0NL
U.K. (🌐)

Graevlerupgaard Frugtplantage
Egsgyden 38, Horne, 5600 Fåborg
Denmark. (🏊)

Ornbaekgaard Frugtplantage
Odenseveh 28, 5853 Orbaek
Denmark. (🏊)

Mellemfolkeligt Samvirke
Meslgade 49, 8000 Arhus
Denmark. (❤)

MSA
Borgergade 10-14, 1300 Copenhagen K
Denmark. (❤)

Job Agencies

National Employment Service

Arbedjdsmarkedsstyrelsen, Blegdamsvej 56
Postbus 2722
2100 Copenhagen Ø
Denmark.

Newspapers

Politiken
Ekstra Bladet
Den Bla Auis
Belingske Tidende
Det Fri Aktuelt
Fryens Stiftstidente
Vestkysten

Help with Travel and Accommodation

Danmark Internationale Studenterkomite
Skindergade 36, 1159 Copenhagen K
Denmark.
(Can also arrange concessionary rates for tours
and entry fees to attractions.)

EGYPT

Author's Comment. Egypt is one of the world's great destinations and well worth a stopover on any trip. It is not the easiest country for the independent traveller to survive in but you can combine it with a stay in Israel—you will discover a great many differences in the culture and lifestyle of these two neighbours. If you do travel to Egypt, take care as there has been some terrorist activity, directed mainly at Western visitors, in recent years.

Jobs You Can Do. Not much choice, but plenty of opportunities to teach English.

What About Daily Life? Cheap living costs, but very low pay. Cairo is a busy, overcrowded city but provides most of what you will need. Other parts of the country can be remote. Egypt (especially Cairo) may be quite westernised in some ways but it is still a Muslim country and you should respect this fact when travelling there.

Entry Regulations. You will need a visa, but there is a lot of unofficial (illegal) work being done.

Job Leads

Arab African Centre for Languages
11 Abdel Khalek Tharwat Street, Downtown, Cairo
Egypt. (✎)
Tel. 574 5635

International Language Centre, Mohamed Bayoumi Street
Heliopolis, Cairo
Egypt. (✎)
Tel. 291 9295

Pegasus Language Centre, Al Salaam Tower, Maadi, Cairo
Egypt (✎).
Tel. 378 1647

Help with Travel and Accommodation

Egyptian Travel Bureau
7 Dr. Abdel Hamid Saiid Street, Maarouf, Cairo
Egypt.
Tel. 02 758099

Egyptian Youth Hostels Association
7 Dr. Abdel Hamid Saiid Street, Maarouf, Cairo
Egypt.
Tel. 02 758099
(International Youth Hostel Federation card holders can obtain
concessionary rates on Egyptian Railways.)

FINLAND

Author's Comment. Finland is a country of forests and lakelands.
Besides the capital city of Helsinki, you will not find many working
opportunities elsewhere. Once work is over, you may want to visit
Lapland in the northern part of the country, or make a side trip into
Russia.

Jobs You Can Do. Some jobs are available in hotels and restaurants
but many working travellers pick up a job on a farm or work as an au
pair (both men and women can work as au pairs here).

What About Daily Life? It is fairly expensive to live here. Wages are
high, but so are the taxes.

Entry Regulations. EU citizens do not need a visa or work permit. Other nationalities do, and they must first find a job, then apply to a Finnish Consulate outside Finland.

Job Leads

KVT
Rauhanasema, Veturitori, 00520 Helsinki 52
Finland. (❤)

Finnish Family Programme
Box 343, 00531 Helsinki
Finland. (⊞, 👫)

Finnish Youth Alliance
Stadion, Etelakaare, 002500 Helsinki
Finland. (👫)

Ministry of Labour
Fabioninkatu 32, PO Box 30, 00100 Helsinki
Finland. (⊞, ⛷, 👫)

Job Agencies

National Employment Agency
Ministry of Labour
P.O. Box 524, Eteläesplanadi 4, 00101 Helsinki
Finland.

Newspapers

Turun Sanomat
Aamulehti
Helsingin Sanomat

Help with Travel and Accommodation

Kompassi
Simonkatu 1, 00100 Helsinki
Finland.
Tel. 612 1863

SRM Travel
Yrjökatu 38 B15, 00100 Helsinki
Finland.
Tel. 694 0377
(Discount of up to 60% on flights, rail travel and car hire.)

FORMER SOVIET UNION

Author's Comment. Fairly new on the working travel scene, the former Soviet Union is mainly for the very adventurous traveller. Distances are vast and most organisations within the region operate in a permanent state of chaos, making it difficult to find a job or accommodation, or arrange for travel within the place or out of it.

Jobs You Can Do. The demand for English teachers is established and growing. You may find a few weeks' work in a hotel, restaurant or office if you are lucky. There are also opportunities for voluntary work.

What About Daily Life? It is cheap enough to get by, but not that cheap, especially in Moscow. Wages are fairly low and only enough to support a basic way of life. If you want any luxuries, you will need to spend your own money.

Most countries of what was once the Soviet Union are now quite open and there is none of the secrecy that characterised life in the past. You are free to go where you want and say what you like. Remember, though, that some of the new countries in the region have political problems and others, such as Russia, are experiencing a problem with organised crime. Many of the countries are developing an identity quite separate from Russia and may shun the Russian language and culture. The main countries that offer work opportunities are Russia, Ukraine, Belarus, Lithuania, Latvia and Estonia.

Entry Regulations. Visas are required for most nationalities. Check before travelling.

Job Leads

ATM
P.O. Box 64, 220119 Minsk
Belarus. (❤)

Austeja
Pylimo 35, 2001 Vilnius
Lithuania. (❤)

Brietner Language School
Sakharova Prospekt, Moscow
Russia. (✎)

Brit-Pol Health Care Foundation
Gerrard House, Worthing Road, East Preston
W. Sussex, BN16 1AW
U.K. (✎)

Centre of Student Activities
Donelaidio 73, Kaunas
Lithuania. (❤)

CSA
Maironio 14-9, Kaunas 3000
Lithuania. (♥)

East European Partnership
317 Putney Bridge Road, London, SW15 2LN
U.K. (♥)

Forum
10 Ternopolskaya, PO Box 10722, 290034 Lvov
Ukraine. (♥)

Intense Language Centre
Ulitsa Gilyarovskogo 31/2 Moscow 125183
Russia. (✎)

International Education Centre
Kutuzovski Prospekt 22, Moscow
Russia. (✎)

International Exchange Centre
2 Republic Square, 226168 Riga
Latvia. (♥)

League of Voluntary Service
Karl Marx Street 40, 22020 Minsk
Belarus. (♥)

Minta
Perkuno al. 4, Kaunas
Lithuania. (✎, 👫)

Mir V Mig
P.O. Box 1085, 310168 Kharkov
Ukraine. (✎)

Polyglot
125 Mira Prospekt, Moscow 129164
Russia. (✎)

Youth Initiative Association
Kolpachny Prospekt 4, 101000 Moscow
Russia. (❤)

Youth Voluntary Service
7/8 Boulevard Komsomolski, Moscow 103982
Russia. (❤)

Help with Travel and Accommodation
Russian Youth Hostels
3rd Sovetskaya Street 28, St. Petersburg 193312
Russia.

FRANCE

Author's Comment. France should be on every working traveller's list. There is so much to see and do that you probably will not manage it all in just one trip. Do not miss both Paris and the Côte d'Azur, although both will make a big dent in your budget!

Jobs You Can Do. If you speak some French, you can always pick up a few days' casual work in bars, restaurants, hotels, shops or farms. Many travellers find work in the Alps in winter, or on campsites in summer, but get there early. There are also plenty of

work as au pairs. Citizens of other EU countries can take up any job they can find, and au pair visas are offered to most other nationalities.

What About Daily Life? France will appeal to all culture lovers, particularly those who enjoy good food, wine and history. The cost of living is not that expensive and you can always find bargains in food, drink and accommodation if you look carefully. Most jobs pay at least a minimum wage. As French employers tend to be a little biased, you will get on much better if you speak some French.

Entry Regulations. EU citizens do not need a visa or work permit. Others must obtain a visa before leaving for France. Residents of former French colonies and au pairs can obtain work permits fairly easily.

Job Leads

Alpotels Agency
P.O. Box 388, London, SW1X 8LW
U.K. (☒,◉)

ANSTJ
17 Avenue Gambetta, 91130 Ris-Orangis
France. (🙌,♥)

Avalon Au Pairs
Thursely House, 53 Station Road, Shalford
Guildford, Surrey, GU4 8HA
U.K. (👫)
Tel. 01483 63640

Blue Water Yacht Crew Agency
La Galerie du Port, 8 Boulevard d'Aguillon, 06600 Antibes
France. (⚠)

Canvas Holidays
12 Abbey Park Place, Dunfermline, Fife, KY12 7PD
U.K. (⚽)

Crystal Holidays
The Courtyard, Arlington Road, Surbiton, KT6 6BW
U.K. (⚽)
Tel. 0181 241 5111

CIDJ
101 Quai Branly, 75740 Paris
France.
(Advice and vacancies for holiday work.)

Club Med
Service Recrutement, Frankrijklei B-2000 Antwerp
Belgium. (✖)

Concordia
27 Rue de Pont Neuf, BP 238, 75024 Paris
France. (♥)

Contiki Holidays
Wells House, 15 Elmfield Road, Bromley, Kent, BR1 1LS
U.K. (⊛)

CPCV
47 Rue de Clichy, 75009 Paris
France. (👫, ❤)

Etudes et Chantiers
8 Boulevard de Strasbourg, 75010 Paris
France. (❤)

European Waterways Ltd.
22 Kingswood Creek, Wraysbury, Staines, Middlesex, TW19 5EN
U.K. (✎, barge crew.)

Inter-Sejours
179 Rue de Courcelles, 75017 Paris
France. (👫)

Jeunesse et Reconstruction
10 Rue de Treviise, 75009 Paris
France. (❤, ⛰)

Maison de Jeunes et de la Culture
25 Rue Marat, 11200 Lezignan
France. (⛰)

MCP
38 Rue de Fauborg St. Denis, 75010 Paris
France. (❤)

Open Access
11 Allée Centrale, Parc Liserb, 06000 Nice
France. (✗)

Peter Insull's Yacht Crew Agency
La Galerie du Port, 8 Boulevard d'Aguillon. 06600 Antibes
France. (⚓)

SCI
129 Rue de Fauborg Poisonnière, 75009 Paris
France. (❤)

Sesame
92 Rue du Dessous des Berges, 75013 Paris
France. (⛵)

Solihull Au Pair Agency
1565 Stratford Road, Hall Green, Birmingham, B28 9JA
U.K. (👪)
Tel. 0121 733 6444

STAJ
27 Rue du Chateau d'eau, 75010 Paris
France. (👫, ❤)

The Au Pair Agency
231 Hale Lane, Edgware, Middlesex, HA8 9QF
U.K. (👪)
Tel. 0181 958 1750

UCPA
62 Rue de la Glaciére, 75640 Paris Cedex 13
France. (👫, ❤)

Universal Care Ltd
Chester House, 9 Windsor End, Beaconsfield, HP9 2JJ
U.K. (👪)
Tel. 01494 678811

UFVC
19 Rue Dareau, 75014 Paris
France. (♦,♥)

Job Agencies

National Employment Service

ANPE
92136 Issy les Moulineaux (offices in all towns)

Private Employment Agencies

Adecco
4 Place de la Défense, 92090 Paris la Défense, France.
Tel. 01 46 98 00 08

Axel
59 Rue des Mathurins, 75008 Paris, France.
Tel. 01 42 66 50 51

Kelly
50 Avenue des Champs Elysees, 75008 Paris, France.
Tel. 01 42 56 44 88

Manpower
9 Rue Jacques Bingen, 75017 Paris, France.
Tel. 01 47 66 03 03

Newspapers

National press
Le Monde
Le Figaro
France-Soir

Regional press
Sud-Ouest (Bordeaux)
La Voix (Lille)
Ouest-France (Rennes)
Le Progrés (Lyon)
La Provençal
La Meridional (Marseille)

English-language newspapers
The News
Dordogne Telegraph
Riviera Reporter

Help with Travel and Accommodation

Fédération Unie des Auberges de Jeunesse
27 rue Pajol, 75018 Paris France.
Tel. 01 46 07 00 01.

GERMANY

Author's Comment. Germany may not be first on everyone's list but is worth a visit. The modern cities of the west contrast sharply with the time-stood-still atmosphere in the east. It is not too hard to find jobs in Germany and serious beer drinkers will be overwhelmed.

Jobs You Can Do. Almost anything, as help is always needed for casual work. If you want to stay longer, consider au pair work (for both men and women).

What About Daily Life? The pay is high but watch the costs of travel and accommodation. You can still have nights out quite cheaply, though. German employers tend to be fair but demanding and will expect you to work hard. Ordinary Germans can seem cool and aloof at first but make an effort to talk to them and they are often very friendly.

Entry Regulations. EU citizens do not need a visa or work permit. Others must have a visa before leaving and should preferably have been resident in another EU country before applying.

Job Leads

Alpotels Agency
P.O. Box 338, London, SW1X 8LX
U.K. (✗, ◉)

Arbeitskreis Freiwillige Soziale Dienste
Stafflenbergstr. 76, 7000 Stuttgart
Germany. (♥)

British Forces Germany
BFG Youth Services, BFPO 140
Germany. (👫)

Bund der Deutschen Katholischen Jugend (BDKJ)
Jugendferienwerk, Antoniusstrasse 3
Postfach 1229, 7314 Wernau/N
Germany. (👫)

Canvas Holidays
12 Abbey Park Place
Dunfermline, Fife, KY12 7PD
U.K. (◉)

Crystal Holidays
The Courtyard, Arlington Road, Surbiton, KT6 6BW
U.K. (◉)
Tel. 0181 241 5111

CFD
Rindeler Starsse 9-11, 6000 Frankfurt-Bornheim 60
Germany. (♥)

Contiki Holidays
Wells House, 15 Elmfield Road, Bromley, Kent, BR1 1LS
U.K. (⊕)

Deutsche Baderverband (Spa Resorts Association)
Schumannstrasse 111, 5300 Bonn 1
Germany. (✕, ⊕)

Deutscher Alpenverein e.V., Praterinsel 5, 8000 Munich 2
Germany. (⊕)

Deutscher Bundesjugendring
Haager Weg 44, 5300 Bonn 1
Germany. (⚥)

FDJ
Unter den Linden 36-38, 1086 Berlin
Germany. (♥)

In Via
Postfach 420, W7800 Freiburg
Germany. (⚤)

International Farm Experience Programme
Stoneleigh Park,
Kenilworth, Warwickshire, CV8 2LG
U.K. (⚱)

Involvement Volunteers Deutschland
Postfach 110224, 3400 Göttingen
Germany. (♥)

LJGD
Kaiserstrasse 43, 5300 Bonn 1
Germany. (♥)

NDF
Auf der Koornerwise 5. 6000 Frankfurt-Am-Main 1
Germany. (♥)

SCI
Blucherstrasse 14, 5300 Bonn 1, Germany. (♥)

Solihull Au Pair Agency
1565 Stratford Road, Hall Green, Birmingham, B28 9JA
U.K. (👪)
Tel. 0121 733 6444

Toc H
National Projects Office, Forest Close, Wendover,
Aylesbury, Bucks, HP22 6BT, U.K. (👫)
Tel. 0296 623911

Universal Care Ltd
Chester House, 9 Windsor End, Beaconsfield, HP9 2JJ
U.K. (👪)
Tel. 01494 678811

Verband Deutscher Freizeitunternehmen e.V., Mittlerer
Steinbachweg 2, Wurzberg
Germany. (🏵)

Willing Workers on Organic Farms
Stettiner Strasse 3, 6301 Pohlheim
Germany. (🌲)

Job Agencies

National Employment Service

Arbeitsamt offices can be found in all towns and the staff are willing
to help foreigners. Those who want to find a job from outside
Germany can write to the government agency:

ZAV
Feuerbachstrasse 42, 6000 Frankfurt Am Main, Germany.

Newspapers

Frankfurter Allgemeine Zeitung
Die Welt
Süddeutsche Zeitung
Bayernkurier
Kölnsiche Rundschau
Weser Kurier
Stuttgarter Zeitung
Berliner Morgenpost

Help with Travel and Accommodation

Deutsches Jugendherbergswerk
Hauptverband, Bismarckstrasse 8
Postfach 1455, 4930 Detmold
Germany.
(German youth hostel association with hostels
in nearly every German town.)

Youth Information Centre
Paul Heysestrasse 22, 80336 Munich
Germany.
(Help and advice on all matters affecting young people.)

GREECE

Author's Comment. Greece is another port of call that should not be missed on a working trip. You can enjoy the beaches and historical monuments during the day, and the food and drink at night. Start your trip in Athens, then 'island hop' by ferry to whichever islands take your fancy. Get there in early summer for the pick of the jobs.

Jobs You Can Do. Almost anything, but most working travellers go for jobs in bars, restaurants or hotels. Fruit-picking jobs are also quite easy to come by as employers often need a few days' help. In Athens, au pairing and nannying are popular. Teaching jobs are also available in private English-language schools, mostly for those with a teaching qualification. There are also some jobs as assistants for those without any teaching qualification.

What About Daily Life? Other than in Athens, it is still fairly cheap to live in Greece. However, do not expect high wages for casual work. The Greeks are generally very friendly but often quite reserved in the rural areas. This contrasts very sharply with the scene in the bustling holiday resorts.

Entry Regulations. EU citizens do not need a visa or work permit. Most other nationalities wishing to work need the necessary documentation, but there is a lot of illegal and unofficial work being done.

Job Leads

Consolas Travel
100 Eolou Street, Athens
Greece.
Tel. 01 325 4931 (⊜)

European Conservation Volunteers
15 Omirou Street, 14562, Kifissia
Greece. (♥)

Euroyouth Ltd
301 Westborough Road, Westcliffe, Southend on Sea
Essex, SS0 9PT
U.K. (♥, ✎)
Tel. 01702 341434

Mark Warner
20 Kensington Church Street, London, W8 4EP
U.K.(⬤)
Tel. 0171 938 1851

Porto Rio Resort
Patras 26001, Greece. (⬤)

SCI
Erika Kalamitzi, 59 Kefallimias Street, 11251 Athens
Greece. (❤)

Students Abroad
36 Whitehorse Street, Baldock, Herts, SG7 6QQ
U.K. (👫)

Sunsail
Port House, Port Solent, Portsmouth, PO6 4TH
U.K.(⬤)
Tel. 01705 214330

Job Agencies

National Employment Service

OAED
Thakris 8, 16610 Glyfada, Athens
Greece.
Tel. 01 993 2589

Regional OAED Offices

Attica and Islands:
Odos Peiraios 52, 10436 Athens.
Tel. 1 5241 113

Peloponnese:
Odos Kanari 54, 262 22 Patra Achaia.
Tel. 61 329 764

Crete:
Plateia Agias Aikaterinis, 711 00 Irakeio Kritis.
Tel. 81 22 345

Macedonia:
Odos Dodekanisou 10A, 540 16 Thessaloniki.
Tel. 31 555 936

Epirus:
3rd Km Ethikis Odou Ioanninon – Athinas, 450 00 Ioannina.
Tel. 651 297 04

East Macedonia & Thrace:
Odos Ethinikis Antistaseos 8, 651 10 Kavala.
Tel. 51 229 688

Thessaly:
Odos Ermogenous 10, 414 47 Larisa.
Tel. 41 535 963

Private Employment Agencies

Athenian Nanny Agency and Domestics
P.O. Box 51181. 14510 Kiffissia, Athens
Greece.
Tel. 301 1303 1005

Camenos International Staff Consultancy
12 Botsai Street, Athens 147
Greece.

Intertom Agency
24-26 Halkokondili Street, Athens 10432
Greece.
Tel. 01 532 9470

Pioneer
11 Nikis Street, Athens 10557
Greece.
Tel. 01 322 4321

Newspapers

English-language
The Athens News
Daily Post
(English newspapers)

HUNGARY

Author's Comment. Hungary must surely count as one of the nicest
eastern European countries. It is surprisingly westernised, but has not
been spoilt by its new links with the West. A visit to Budapest is a
must, but do plan to spend some time in the provinces with, perhaps,
a visit to Lake Balaton.

Jobs You Can Do. Almost anything you can get. Most working
travellers opt for the teaching of English. There are some opportunities for au pairs and plenty of openings for voluntary work.

What About Daily Life? Hungary will not overstretch your budget
but it is getting pricier to live there. You can get most Western goods
quite easily so you will not feel cut off.

Entry Regulations. Europeans and Americans do not need a visa for time spent as a tourist, or to work on voluntary projects. Others should check. If you want to work you will need a work permit, although some occupations are exempt from this.

Job Leads

Aaron Employment Agency
The Courtyard, Stanley Road, Tunbridge Wells
Kent, TN1 2RJ
U.K. (🛉)
Tel. 01892 546601

Biokultura
MBKEE, Toroku 7, Budapest 1023
Hungary. (🌄)

Brit-Pol Health Care Foundation
Gerrard House, Worthing Road, East Preston, W. Sussex
U.K. (✎)

English Teachers Foundation
Dozsa Gyorgy Utca 104, 1068 Budapest
Hungary. (✎)

East European Partnership
317 Putney Bridge Road, London, SW15 2LN
U.K. (♥)

Hungarian Chamber of Language Schools
Rath Gyorgy Utca 24, 1122 Budapest
Hungary. (✎)

KISZ
P.O. Box 72, 1388 Budapest
Hungary. (❤)

Teach Hungary Programme
175 High Street, Belfast, Maine
U.S.A. (✎)

Unio Youth Workcamps Association
Xun. B, pkp 37-38, 1138
Budapest
Hungary. (❤)

Job Agencies

National Employment Services

Katona J. Utca 25, Budapest.
Tel. 1 122 294

Bokány D. Utca 2a, Budapest.
Tel. 1 124 630

Széchenyi Ter 9, Pécs.
Tel. 72 13 721

Bajcsy Zs. Utca 4, Szeged.
Tel. 62 22 890

Csaba Utca 26, Györ.
Tel. 96 11 180

Help with Travel and Accommodation

International Bureau for Youth Tourism & Exchange (BITEJ)
Ady E Utca, 1024 Budapest
Hungary.

Express Travel Bureau
1395 Budapest V. Szabadsag Ter. 16
Hungary.
Tel. 01 153 0660

INDIAN SUB-CONTINENT

Author's Comment. Travelling through India is one of the great travel experiences in the world. Go by train; despite the crowds and chaos, it is the best way to see everything there is to see. Bombay and Goa are both well worth the time and effort.

Jobs You Can Do. Foreigners do not have many work opportunities. Voluntary work is available, but it is best if you have a skill to offer (for example, teaching or nursing). In a city, you may get yourself a few days' work teaching English, or working on some project in an office.

What About Daily Life? Inexpensive, so you probably do not need to work. Can be very basic with few or no modern conveniences, especially outside cities. Remember that India is a massive country which encompasses many different cultures and languages, so you will need to adapt to the local situation wherever you may find yourself.

Entry Regulations. Check latest position before travelling. Most nationalities need a visa to visit India, Pakistan, Bangladesh and Sri Lanka. A work visa or permit is unnecessary for most nationalities in India (for short stays only).

Job Leads

Bangladesh Work Camps Association
289/2 Work Camps Road, North Shahjahanpur, Dhaka 17
Bangladesh. (❤)

Help
60 The Pleasance, Edinburgh, EH8 9JT
U.K. (❤)

Indian Volunteers for Community Service
12 Eastleigh Avenue, Harrow, Middlesex
U.K. (❤)

Joint Assistance Centre
H65 South Extension 1, New Delhi
India. (❤)

SCI
K5 Green Park, New Delhi 110016
India. (❤)

Sri Lanka Jatika Sarvodaya Shramadana Sangamaya Inc.
98 Rawatawatta Road, Moratuwa
Sri Lanka. (❤)

Help with Travel and Accommodation

Bangladesh Youth Hostel Association
42/2 Azimpur Road, Dhaka 1205
Bangladesh.
Tel. 503445

National Youth Hostel Association of Sri Lanka
26 Charlemont Road, Colombo 6
Sri Lanka.
Tel. 584303

Nepal Youth Hostels Association
Mahendra Youth Hostel, Jawalakhel, Lalitpur
Nepal.
Tel. 21003

Pakistan Youth Hostels Association
Garden Road, Aabpara, Sector G-6/4, Islamabad
Pakistan.
Tel. 826899

Youth Hostels Association of India
5 Nyaya Marg, Chankyapuri, New Delhi 110021
India.
Tel. 301 1969

IRELAND (REPUBLIC OF)

Author's Comment. Not often a port of call for a working holiday, but good for those looking for a laid-back way of life and friendly people. Job opportunities are limited, however, as unemployment is quite high.

Jobs You Can Do. Almost anything, if you can get any job offer. Try au pairing, or how about a couple of weeks' work on a conservation project?

What About Daily Life? Ireland can be a bit expensive to live in, especially compared with the U.K. Most casual jobs do not pay much.

Entry Regulations. EU citizens do not need a visa or a work permit. (British citizens do not even need a passport.) Other nationalities should check the requirements with their nearest Irish Embassy. U.S. and Canadian students can obtain a Working Holiday Visa.

Job Leads

COMCHAIRDEAS
3 Montague Street, Dublin 2
Ireland. (❤)

Community and Youth Information Centre
Sackville House,
Sackville Place, Dublin 1
Ireland. (❤)

Langtrain International
Torquay Road, Foxrock, Dublin 18
Ireland. (👫)
Tel. 1 289 3879

Simon Community
P.O. Box 1022, Dublin 1
Ireland. (❤)

VSI
37 North Great George Street, Dublin 1
Ireland. (❤)

Willing Workers on Organic Farms
Crowhill, Newgrove, Tulla, Co. Clare
Ireland. (🏕)

Job Agencies

FÁS (National Employment Service)
65a Adelaide Road
Dublin 2
Ireland.
Tel. 01 765861
(Has offices in most Irish towns.)

Private Employment Agencies

Get a list of this from the National Employment Service (see the address above).

Newspapers

The Irish Independent
The Irish Times
The Irish Press

Help with Travel and Accommodation

Community & Youth Information Centre
Sackville House, Sackville Place, Dublin 1
Ireland.
Tel. 1 878 6844

Irish Youth Hostel Association
Travel Section, 39 Mountjoy Square, Dublin 1
Ireland.
Tel. 01 363111
(Discounts on a wide range of travel and ferry services.)

ISRAEL

Author's Comment. Israel offers a sharp cultural contrast with its Arab neighbours. In Israel, you can enjoy the history and culture of the Middle East alongside Western influences like fast food and American television programmes.

Jobs You Can Do. Most jobs available officially are on kibbutzim or moshavim (collective farms), although there is some illegal work being done in hotels and bars. There are plenty of opportunities for au pairs and voluntary work on historic sites.

What About Daily Life? Although Israel appears westernised, it is a strict Jewish society. The country can be quite expensive and most voluntary positions pay only a small amount of pocket money.

Entry Regulations. All visitors need a visa and, if there is any intention to work, a work permit. You should make arrangements for your job before arrival.

Job Leads

Au Pair International
2 Desler Street, Bnei Brak 51507
Israel.
Tel. 03 619 0423 (🕴)

Israel Antiquities Authority
P.O. Box 586, Jerusalem 91004
Israel. (❤)

Jewish National Fund
11 Zvi Shapira Street, Tel Aviv 64538
Israel. (❤)

Kibbutz Program Center
Volunteer Department, 124 Hayarkon Street, Tel Aviv 63573
Israel.

Kibbutz Representatives
1a Accommodation Road, London, NW11 8ED
U.K.
Tel. 0181 458 9235

Kibbutz Representatives
110 East 59th Street, New York
U.S.A.
Tel. 212 318 6130

Star Au Pairs
16 Michal Street, Tel Aviv 63261
Israel. (🕴)
Tel. 03 291748

Students Abroad
36 Whitehorse Street, Baldock, Herts, SG7 6QQ
U.K. (⊞)

Help with Travel and Accommodation

Israel Students Tourist Association
109 Ben Yehuda Street, Tel Aviv 63401
Israel.

Israel Youth Hostel Association
P.O. Box 1075, Jerusalem 91009
Israel.
Tel. 02 252706

Newspaper

Jerusalem Post (English-language)

ITALY

Author's Comment. Italy is a wonderful country to travel through, offering a pleasant climate and warm, friendly people, plus all the food and drink you can make room for. However, work opportunities are more limited than in other European countries, especially if you do not speak Italian. There is also a big difference between the prosperous, industrious north and the slower, more sleepy south.

Jobs You Can Do. Anything you can get. There are plenty of vacancies for au pairs. Many working travellers are attracted to jobs in the ski resorts in winter.

147

What About Daily Life? Can be expensive, especially in the north, but you can get good food and accommodation at a reasonable price in most places.

Entry Regulations. EU citizens do not need a visa or work permit. Other nationalities will need a visa if there is any intention to work.

Job Leads

Associazione Italiana Sociostruttori
Via Cesare Battisti 3, 20071 Casalpusterlengo, Milan
Italy. (❤)

Au Pair International
Via San Stefano 32, 40125 Bologna
Italy. (👫)

Au Pairs Italy
46 The Rise, Sevenoaks, Kent, TN13 1RJ
U.K. (⚲)
Tel. 01732 451522

Avalon Au Pairs
Thursely House, 53 Station Road, Shalford
Guildford. Surrey, GU4 8HA
U.K. (⚲)
Tel. 01483 63640

British Institutes
Via Matteotti 34, 18038 San Remo
Italy. (⚲)
Tel. 0184 506070

Canvas Holidays
12 Abbey Park Place, Dunfermline, Fife, KY12 7PD
U.K. (⚲)

Crystal Holidays
The Courtyard, Arlington Road, Surbiton, KT6 6BW
U.K. (⚲)
Tel. 0181 241 5111

Contiki Holidays
Wells House, 15 Elmfield Road, Bromley, Kent, BR1 1LS
U.K. (⚲)

Family Links s.a.s.
Via Madonnelle, 81020 Puccianiello, Caserta
Italy. (⚲)

Gruppi Archeologici d'Italia
Via Tacito 41, 00193 Rome
Italy. (♥)

MCP
Via Rattazi 24, 000181 Rome
Italy. (♥)

SCI
Via del Laterani 28, 00181 Rome
Italy. (♥)

The Au Pair Agency
231 Hale Lane, Edgware, Middlesex, HA8 9QF
U.K. (👫)
Tel. 0181 958 1750

Universal Care Ltd
Chester House, 9 Windsor End, Beaconsfield, HP9 2JJ
U.K. (👫)
Tel. 01494 678811

Job Agencies

National Employment Service

Ufficio di Collocaménto
Mandòpera, Via Pastrengo 16, Rome
Italy.

Newspapers

Il Massaggero
Corriere della Sera
La Repubblica
La Voce Repubblicana (Rome)
La Nazione (Florence)
Corriere della Serra

Il Giornale (Milan)
La Stampa (Turin)
Il Giornale di Napoli (Naples)
Il Gazzetino (Venice)

Help with Travel and Accommodation

Youth and Student Travel Service
Via Zanetti 18, 50123 Florence
Italy.

JAPAN

Author's Comment. No matter where you are travelling from, Japan will give you culture shock in a big way. The country is a fascinating combination of old and new. You will probably want to start in Tokyo but do not miss a visit to the ancient capital of Kyoto, and also to Hiroshima.

Jobs You Can Do. There is not much choice unless you speak fluent Japanese, but you can try for a job as an English-language teacher. There are also a few opportunities for voluntary work.

What About Daily Life? Japan is expensive. You will need a sizeable emergency fund to pay for a trip here, especially if you are not working. Accommodation is difficult to find. Japanese society may look westernised, especially in the big cities, but slip behind those front doors and you will find that customs and traditions dating back thousands of years are still very important to the people.

Entry Regulations. You will need a visa if you plan to work. This can be obtained from the Japanese Consulate in your own country after you have been offered a job.

151

Job Leads

Japan Exchange & Teaching Programme
CIEE, 33 Seymour Place, London, W1H 6AT
U.K. (✎)
Tel. 0171 224 8896

Japan Exchange & Teaching Programme
Japanese Embassy, 2520 Massachusetts Avenue NW
Washington DC20008
U.S.A. (✎)
Tel. 202 234 2266

Japanese Association of Language Teachers
8 Sumitoma Seimei Building, Shimoyogo-ku, Tokyo
Japan. (✎)

NICE
501 Viewcity, 2-2-1 Shinjuku, Shinjuku-ku, Tokyo 160
Japan. (❤)

Selected Language Schools teaching English

ICA
1-16-10 Nishi Ikebukuro, Toyoshima-ku
Tokyo.

ECC
1-5-4 Kabuki-cho, Shinjuku-ku
Tokyo.

Berlitz School of Languages
1-11-41 Akasaka, Chiyoda-ku
Tokyo.

GGG
1-14-16 Jugoaka, Meguro-ku
Tokyo 4-60.

Executive Gogaku Centre
1-21-2 Yutenji, Meguro-ku
Tokyo.

Stanton School of English
Rokuban 7 chome, Chiyoda-ku
Tokyo.

ANR
7-2 Marunouchi 1 chome, Chiyoda-ku
Tokyo.

Gaigo Semmon Gakko Osaka
2-5 Shimmamachi, Higashi-ku
Osaka.

Business Gakko
13-1 Nanba-naka, Nanlwa-ku
Osaka.

Tokyo Gogaku Academy
2-15-14 Kamiosaki, Shinagawa-ku
Tokyo.

Brittania Gaigo Gakuin
3-3-1 Ayase, Adachi-ku
Tokyo.

HJK Academy
2-1-3 Nishi-Shinjuku, Shinjuku-ku
Tokyo.

Cosmopolitan Language Institute
Yoshima B Building, 8-9 Yaesu i chome, Chuo-ku
Tokyo 4-61.

Commons Language School
506 Tokokumi Building, 27-12 Hon-cho 6 chome, Nakano-ku
Tokyo.

Idibashi Foreign Language Institute
7-11 Fujimi 2 chome, Minato-ku
Tokyo.

Roppongi Language School
1-19 Roppongi 4 chome, Minato-ku
Tokyo.

WIZ Language Institute
20-8 Oasaki 1 chome, Shinagawa-ku
Tokyo.

Shinuya Language School
15-15 Sakunagaoka-machi, Shinuya-ku
Tokyo.

Bilingual
21-25 Akasaka 2 chome, Minato-ku
Tokyo.

Bilingual
3-4 Sonezaki Shinchi 2 chome, Kita-ku
Osaka.

Newspapers

Japan Times (English-language).

Help with Travel and Accommodation

Student Association of Japan
Kokusai Kyoiku, Shinko-kai, 1-21 Yotsuja
Shinjuku-ku, Tokyo 160
Japan.

LATIN AMERICA

Author's Comment. A trip into Latin America should definitely be on the cards for the adventurous traveller. With its political problems and chaotic travel arrangements, anything can happen here—and probably will. Both Mexico and Brazil are highlights of any Latin American trip.

Jobs You Can Do. The teaching of English is the main way of earning a living legally. Voluntary work is available. Other jobs may be offered on an unofficial basis, but are poorly paid.

What About Daily Life? It is quite inexpensive to travel and live in Latin America, but the cities can be costly. Make sure you are well insured (see Chapter Three) and have a sizeable emergency fund.

Entry Regulations. As situations vary from country to country, it is important to check with the relevant embassy or consulate.

Job Leads

American Friends Service Committee
1501 Cherry Street, Philadelphia, PA19102-1479
U.S.A. (♥)

Amigos de las Americas
5618 Star Lane, Houston, TX77057
U.S.A. (❤)

AMISTOUR
Versalles 35-502, 06600, Mexico City
Mexico. (❤)

ELS International Corp.
5761 Buckingham Parkway, Culver City
California, CA90230
U.S.A. (✎)
Tel. 310 642 0982

Journey Latin America
16 Devonshire Road, London, W4 2HH
U.K. (✎)

Los Ninõs
1330 Continental Street, San Ysidro, CA92073
U.S.A. (❤)

Nature Conservancy Association
1800 North Kent Street, Suite 800
Arlington, VA22209
U.S.A. (❤)

SETEJ
Hamburgo 301, Col. Juarez, 06600 Mexico City
Mexico. (❤)

Help with Travel and Accommodation

Each of the following operates youth hostels in their own country.

Asociación Argentina de Albergues de la Juventud
Talcahuano 214 2-6, 1013 Buenos Aires
Argentina.
Tel. 45 1001/2537

Federacão Brazileira dos Albergues de Juventude
Rua da Assemléia 10, S1211 Centro
CEP 20119, Rio de Janeiro
Brazil.
Tel. 21 252 4829

Asociación Chilena de Albergues Turisticos Juveniles
Avenida Providencia 2594, OF420-421
Providencia, Santiago
Chile.
Tel. 233 3220

Albergues de Colombia para el Mundo
P.O. Box 3220, Carrera 7, No. 6-10, Bogota
Colombia.
Tel. 91 280 3318

CONADE
Comisión Nacional del Deporte
Dirección de Villas Deportivas Juveniles
Glorieta del Metro Insurgentes, Local C-11
Col. Juarez, CP06600, Mexico City DF
Mexico.
Tel. 525 2974

Asociación Peruana de Albergues Juveniles
Casimro Ulloa 328, San Antonio
Miraflores, Lima 18
Peru.
Tel. 46 5488

Asociación de Alberguistas del Uruguay
Pablo de Maria 1538/008
11200 Montevideo
Uruguay.
Tel. 404245

MIDDLE EAST

See individual headings for information on Egypt and Israel.

Author's Comment. The Middle Eastern countries are not popular with working travellers. This is due mainly to the religious climate and restricted way of life (especially for women). There is also a lack of things to see and do. Egypt and Israel (covered elsewhere in this section) are more interesting destinations, while Dubai is becoming quite popular as a tourist spot.

Jobs You Can Do. There are not many opportunities. The most common are the teaching of English, nannying and jobs in business or commerce (if skilled and experienced).

What About Daily Life? Most countries are quite expensive and there is not a lot to see and do. Visitors to all countries should remember the religious situation which exists, restricting many aspects of daily life and personal behaviour, especially for women.

Entry Regulations. Most countries require a visa, even for tourists.

158

Job Leads

Park Lane Nannies
22 Upper Maudlin Street, Bristol, BS2 8DJ
U.K. (👪)
Tel. 0117 922 6237

Stable Relief Service
The Old Rectory, Belton in Rutland, Uppingham
Leicestershire, LE15 9LE
U.K. (🏕, 👪)
Tel. 01572 86381

Newspapers

Home & Away
Expats House, 29 Lacon Road, London, SE22 9HE
U.K.

Resident Abroad
Greystoke Place, Fetter Lane, London, EC2A 1ND
U.K.

(Both publications list vacancies in the Middle East, mainly for those with business and technical skills and experience.)

NETHERLANDS

Author's Comment. The Netherlands is a friendly country where it is quite easy to find casual work for a few days, and at good rates too. Everyone heads for Amsterdam, which is where you will probably want to start as it offers a great social life. However, jobs are often easier to come by in the less-visited provinces. The country is great for cyclists too.

Jobs You Can Do. Hotels, bars, shops, farms and building sites are always in need of casual staff. Any private employment agency should have something to offer you, even if you do not speak Dutch. There are also plenty of au pair jobs.

What About Daily Life? The Netherlands is not too expensive to live in and wages are good. If you are below the age of 23, you are not entitled to the same rates of pay as older people. This may turn out to your advantage because employers will prefer to hire you.

Entry Regulations. EU citizens do not need a visa or work permit to get a job in the Netherlands. Others will need a work permit to take up a job. The employer will put in the application for you.

Job Leads

Au Pair & Activity International
Postbus 7097, 9701 JB Groningen
Netherlands. (👪)

Avalon Au Pairs
Thursely House, 53 Station Road, Shalford
Guildford, Surrey, GU4 8HA
U.K. (👪)
Tel. 01483 63640

Baartmaan & Koning
P.O. Box 27, 2170 AA Sassenheim
Netherlands. (🌾)

Central Bureau Arbeidsvoorziening
P.O. Box 437, 2280 AR, Rijswijk
Netherlands.
(Can recommend and advise on temporary work for young people, in all types of industry.)

Eurocamp Plc
Knutsford, Cheshire WA16 0NL
U.K. (⊛)

HRC International
St. Maartenslaan 26, 6221 AX Maastricht
Netherlands. (☒)

ICVD
Postbus 377, 1000 AJ Amsterdam
Netherlands. (♥)

International Farm Experience Programme
Stoneleigh Park, Kenilworth, Warwickshire, CV8 2LG
U.K. (⛲)

North South Agency
28 Wellington Road, Hastings. E. Sussex, TN34 3RN
U.K. (♟)
Tel. 01424 422364

SIW
Willemstraat 7, 3511 RJ Utrecht
Netherlands. (♥)

Students Abroad
36 Whitehorse Street, Baldock, Herts, SG7 6QQ
U.K. (♟)

The Au Pair Agency
231 Hale Lane, Edgware, Middlesex, HA8 9QF
U.K. (♟)
Tel. 0181 958 1750

VIA
Bethanienstraat 20, 1012 CA Amsterdam
Netherlands. (❤)

Job Agencies

National Employment Service

Singel 202
1016 AA Amsterdam.
Tel. 020 520 0911

Begynenhof 8, 5611 EL Eindhoven.
Tel. 040 325325

Engelse Kamp 4, 9722 AX Groningen.
Tel. 050 225911

Troelstrakade 65, 2531 AA The Hague.

Schiedamse Vest 160, 3011 BH Rotterdam.

Private Employment Agencies
Manpower
Van Baerlestraat 16, Amsterdam
Netherlands.
Tel. 020 664 4180

Randstad
Postbus 12600 1100 AP Amsterdam Zuid-Oost
Netherlands.
Tel. 020 569 5911

Newspapers

De Telegraaf
De Volkskrant
Het Parool (Amsterdam)
Haagsche Courant (The Hague)
Utrechts Nieuwsblad (Utrecht)

Help with Travel and Accommodation

NBBS Travel has information centres in most cities and large towns. Its head office is at

Schipolweg 101
2300 AJ Leiden.

NEW ZEALAND

Author's Comment. A quiet, peaceful country which is not cheap to travel to. If you plan to visit, it may be best to make it a stopover on a round-the-world air ticket. The place is great if you are looking for solitude and a relaxing atmosphere.

Jobs You Can Do. There is usually casual work on farms, depending on the season. Some jobs are also available in offices and shops, and working travellers sometimes find work on yachts.

What About Daily Life? Once you are in the country, the cost of living is not too high. However, the place may be too quiet for some people. Visitors from the U.K. and Australia always feel at home.

Entry Regulations. You can travel to New Zealand, find a job, and then apply for a working visa. However, there is no guarantee that it will be granted. Young people aged between 18 and 30 from certain countries (including the U.K. and the Netherlands) can apply to the Working Holiday Scheme starting from May 1 each year. If you are accepted, the scheme entitles you to travel to New Zealand first, and then get a job. The maximum stay is 12 months.

Job Leads

International Agricultural Exchange Association
Stoneleigh Park, Kenilworth, Warwickshire, CV8 2LG
U.K. (☷)

GAP Activity Projects
Queens Road, Reading, RG1 4BB
U.K.
Tel. 01734 594914 (✎)

Involvement Volunteers Association
P.O. Box 218, Port Melbourne, VIC 3207
Australia. (♥)

Willing Workers on Organic Farms
P.O. Box 10037 Palmerston
North, North Island
New Zealand. (☷)

Job Agencies

Adia Personnel
New Zealand.
Tel. 04 472 9115

Drake
Scollay House, 5-7 Willeston Street, Wellington
New Zealand.
Tel. 04 472 6972

Kelly Services
DB Tower, 111 The Terrace, Wellington
New Zealand.
Tel. 01 499 2825

Student Job Search (SJS)
P.O. Box 9193 Wellington, New Zealand.
Tel. 04 471 1967

Help with Travel and Accommodation

New Zealand University Students Association
Travel Bureau, PO Box 6368, Te Aro, Wellington
New Zealand.

Youth Hostel Association of New Zealand
P.O. Box 436, Christchurch 1
New Zealand.
Tel. 3799 970
(Members enjoy discounts on accommodation, travel,
entertainment and shopping.)

NORWAY

Author's Comment. As a fairly sparsely populated country, Norway does not have many job vacancies. However, since it is quite an expensive country to travel in, you will probably want to pick up a few days' work to supplement your funds. Oslo is a bustling city and the coastal ferry trip up to Nordkapp is one of the world's great journeys.

Jobs You Can Do. There are a few jobs in hotels and restaurants, plus au pairing and work on the farms in summer. The shipyards also employ casual staff.

What About Daily Life? Norway can be expensive, but wages are quite high. Be prepared for very cold weather in winter.

Entry Regulations. EU citizens do not need a visa or work permit, although Norway is not a member of the EU. Other nationalities will need a work visa which must be obtained through a Norwegian Consulate before leaving for Norway.

Job Leads

Avalon Au Pairs
Thursely House, 53 Station Road, Shalford
Guildford. Surrey, GU4 8HA
U.K. (⚄)
Tel. 01484 63640

Eurocamp Plc
Knutsford, Cheshire WA16 0NL
U.K. (⚈)

Internasjonal Dugnad
Langesgate 6, 0165 Oslo 1
Norway. (♥)

The Norwegian Foundation for Youth Exchange
Rolf Hofmosgate 18, 0655 Oslo l
Norway. (♥, ⚄, ⊞, ⛷)

The Solihull Au Pair & Nanny Agency
1565 Stratford Road, Hall Green
Birmingham, B28 9JA
U.K. (⚄)
Tel. 0121 733 6444

Job Agencies

National Employment Service

Arbeidsdirektoratet
Postboks 8127 Dep, Oslo 00332
Norway.
Tel. 22 94 24 00

Employment Service Green Line
Tel. 800 33166 (Free service in Norway only.)

Newspapers

Dagbladet
Aftenposten
Arbeiderbladet

Help with Travel and Accommodation

Norwegian Student Travel Office
P.O. Box 55, Oslo 3
Norway.

POLAND

Author's Comment. Poland does not attract many travellers. Most people wanting to explore eastern Europe head for the Czech Republic or Hungary. While Poland may not have as much character as those countries, it does have friendly people. Do not spend all your time in the industrial centres of Warsaw and Katowice/Krakow; there are many pleasant suburban towns, especially in the Tatra mountains.

Jobs You Can Do. The teaching of English is the main choice. There are also a few jobs in tourism. There are lots of opportunities for voluntary work but you will have to pay for your stay.

167

What About Daily Life? Poland is cheap, but you will be hard-pressed to show much profit, even from a job that pays fairly well. Some of the cities are a bit depressing.

Entry Regulations. Most nationalities can stay as tourists for up to 90 days without a visa (U.K. citizens can remain for up to six months). You will have to get a visa if you plan to work. Check the details with the nearest Polish Consulate.

Job Leads

Almatur
Ul. Ordynacka 9, 00364 Warsaw
Poland. (✖,◉)

Anglo Polish Academic Association
93 Victoria Road, Leeds, LS6 1DR
U.K. (✎)

East European Partnership
317 Putney Bridge Road, London, SW15 2LN
U.K. (❤)

Foundation for International Youth Exchanges (FIYE),
Ul. Grzybowska 79, 00844 Warsaw
Poland. (❤)

Camptur
Ul. Krolewska 27, 00600 Warsaw
Poland. (✖,◉)

Gromada
Ul. Podwale 23, 00962 Warsaw
Poland. (✖,◉)

Harctur Co. Ltd.
Ul. Niemcewicza 17, 00973 Warsaw
Poland. (✖, ⊛)

OHP
Bowy Swiat 18/20, 00920 Warsaw
Poland. (❤)

Orbis
Ul. Bracka 16, 00028 Warsaw
Poland. (✖, ⊛)

Pegrotour SA
Ul. Bertholda Brechta 3, 03472 Warsaw
Poland. (✖, ⊛)

Sports-Tourist
Ul. Grochowska 280, 00987 Warsaw
Poland. (✖, ⊛)

Newspaper

Warsaw Gazette

Help with Travel and Accommodation

Almatur
Ul. Kopernike 15, 00364 Warsaw
Poland.

Junior Travel Agency
Ul. Chocimska 28, 00791 Warsaw
Poland.

Polskie Towarzystwo Schronisk
Mlodziezowych, Ul. Chocimska 28, 00791 Warsaw
Poland.

PORTUGAL

Author's Comment. Portugal is a great country to travel through as it is uncrowded, friendly and fairly cheap. You can still spend weeks on the Algarve's golden beaches for comparatively little money. However, not many jobs are available.

Jobs You Can Do. Most jobs are in the tourist industry in summer (May-September). There are also voluntary work projects, au pairing and a few jobs on farms.

What About Daily Life? Portugal is inexpensive to live in but do not expect high wages. Although the seaside resorts attract many tourists in summer, rural Portugal is very quiet and traditional. The people are staunchly Catholic.

Entry Regulations. EU citizens do not need a work permit or visa. Other nationalities will need a work permit, which the employer will obtain on your behalf.

Job Leads

ATEJ
P.O. Box 4586, 4009 Porto
Portugal. (♥)

Centro de Intercambio e Turismo Universatario
Av. Defensores de Chaves, 67-6 Dto, Lisbon
Portugal. (👥)

Companheiros Construtores
Rua Pedro Monteiro 3-1, 3000 Coimbra
Portugal. (❤)

Critaos Para A Paz
Rua Citade de Poitiers 44-1, Montel Formosa, 3000 Coimbra
Portugal. (❤)

Euroyouth
301 Westborough Road, Westcliff, Southend on Sea,
Essex, SS0 9PT
U.K. (✎)
Tel. 01702 341434

Instituto da Juventude
Avenida Duque d'Avilia 137, 1000 Lisbon
Portugal. (❤)

Job Agencies

Ministério de Trabalho
Praça de Londres, 1091 Lisbon Codex
Portugal.

Newspapers

Correio de Manha
O Diario
Diario (Lisbon)
Jornal de Noticias (Oporto)

English-language newspapers
Anglo-Portuguese News
Madeira Island Bulletin

Help with Travel and Accommodation

Turicoop
Rua Pascal de Melo 15-1, 1100 Lisbon
Portugal.
(Can arrange inexpensive accommodation for young people.)

ROMANIA

Author's Comment. Romania is not the easiest country for the working holidaymaker to survive in. The country is severely run down and there is not much money to pay foreigners to get work done. On the positive side, Romania has friendly people and lovely countryside—you can even visit Transylvania and look up Count Dracula in his palace!

Jobs You Can Do. These are mostly in voluntary projects. There is a small number of teaching jobs and a few companies promoting holiday packages require staff (mainly for ski holidays).

What About Daily Life? Cheap enough, but quite basic. Be prepared to encounter much poverty and do not expect any luxuries.

Entry Regulations. All nationalities need a visa for any kind of trip, whether or not work is involved.

Job Leads

IVS
Old Hall, East Bergholt, Colchester, Essex, CO7 6TQ
U.K. (♥)

Crystal Holidays
Crystal House, The Courtyard, Arlington Road
Surbiton, Surrey, KT6 6BW
U.K. (☻)
Tel. 0181 241 5111 (☻)

East Anglian Appeal for Romania
5 Faversham Road, Beckenham, Kent, BR3 3PN
U.K. (♥)
Tel. 0181 658 9207

Ministry of Education
Strada Berthelot 30, 70749 Bucharest
Romania. (✎)

Operation Romanian Villages
54 Waldemar Avenue, London, SW6 5NA
U.K. (♥)
Tel. 0171 731 4133

SLOVAK REPUBLIC

Author's Comment. One of the smallest eastern European countries formed in 1993 after Czechoslovakia was divided, it is very much a quiet, rural country. If you are in Vienna (Austria), it is easy enough to go over to Bratislava, capital of the Slovak Republic, for a day or two.

Jobs You Can Do. Mostly the teaching of English, or voluntary work.

What About Daily Life? Inexpensive. Bratislava is a bit of a backwater where things to do and places to see are concerned.

173

Entry Regulations. Check before travelling, but most nationalities do not need a visa for a short stay as a tourist.

Job Leads

Academic Information Agency
Hviezdoslavovo Namesti 14, 81000 Bratislava
Slovak Republic. (✎)

East European Partnership
317 Putney Bridge Road, London, SW15 2LN
U.K. (❤)

Inex
Prazska 11, 81104 Bratislava
Slovak Republic. (❤)

Help with Travel and Accommodation

Slovak Academic Information Agency
Hviezdoslavovo Namesti 14, 81000 Bratislava
Slovak Republic.

SOUTH AFRICA

Author's Comment. Now that South Africa has been accepted into the international community, it has become a 'must see' destination for travellers. It is slowly becoming cheaper to get to South Africa, and to stay there too. Make sure you spend some time in Cape Town.

Jobs You Can Do. There is plenty of work available in offices, hotels, restaurants and bars, as well as in nursing and teaching, but you will probably have to apply for a visa to be able to get the jobs. There is also quite a lot of unofficial (illegal) work being done. Those prepared to do voluntary work will find lots of opportunities.

What About Daily Life? South Africa is more expensive than other African countries, especially for accommodation, food and entertainment. Still, it is fairly reasonable by international standards. Although South Africa is now a fully democratic country, there have been some problems with crime and violence in the past few years, so take care when travelling.

Entry Regulations. You will need a work permit in order to work legally, and this may be hard to obtain.

Job Agencies

Browns Personnel Consultants (Pty) Ltd
Box 757, Cramerview
2060 South Africa

Contact Personnel
301a Exchange Building, 28 St. George's Mall, Capetown
South Africa.

Grab a Student (Pty) Ltd
3rd Floor, The Waverley, Winchester Street, Mowbray, Capetown
South Africa.

Newspapers

The Argus
The Star
The Citizen

Help with Travel and Accommodation

South African Youth Hostel Association
P.O. Box 4402, Cape Town 8000, South Africa.
Tel. 419 1853

SPAIN

Author's Comment. Spain offers a lot of potential for the working traveller. There are plenty of jobs in the bustling tourist industry during the summer months. Besides the golden coastline of mainland Spain, do not forget the Balearic and Canary Islands which attract thousands of visitors. If you are looking for culture, head inland and visit Barcelona, Seville or Granada.

Jobs You Can Do. Most working travellers find work in the tourist industry, but get there at the start of the season and be determined. There are lots of jobs but strong competition as well. There are also opportunities for au pairs, voluntary workers and some jobs on farms if you do not mind the blazing Spanish sun.

What About Daily Life? Living costs are cheap inland. Expenses are higher in the tourist resorts but it is still possible to get bargains in food, accommodation and travel.

Entry Regulations. EU citizens do not need a visa or work permit. Other nationalities wishing to work need a visa to travel to Spain.

Job Leads

Aaron Employment Agency
The Courtyard, Stanley Road, Tunbridge Wells, Kent, TN1 2RJ
U.K. (🏃)
Tel. 01892 546601

Association of Language Teaching Institutions
Calle Sagasta 27, 28004 Madrid
Spain. (✎)

Avalon Au Pairs
Thursely House, 53 Station Road, Shalford
Guildford, Surrey, GU4 8HA, U.K. (🏃)
Tel. 01483 63640

British Council
Santa Barbara 10, 28004 Madrid
Spain. (✎)

Canvas Holidays
12 Abbey Park Place, Dunfermline, Fife, KY12 7PD.
U.K. (⊕)

Crystal Holidays
The Courtyard, Arlington Road, Surbiton, KT6 6BW
U.K. (⊕)
Tel. 0181 241 5111

Centros Europes
Calle Principe 12, 28012 Madrid
Spain. (✎)

Club de Relaciones Culturales Internacionales
Calle de Feraz 82, 28008 Madrid
Spain. (♥)

Escuelas Berlitz
Gran Via 80, 28013 Madrid
Spain. (✎)

Eurocamp Plc
Knutsford, Cheshire WA16 0NL
U.K. (⊕)

Euroyouth Ltd
301 Westborough Road, Westcliff, Southend on Sea
Essex, SS0 9PT
U.K. (✎)
Tel. 01702 341434

Instituto de la Juventud
José y Gasset 71, 28006 Madrid
Spain. (❤)

Melia Hotels
Calle Princessa 27, 28008 Madrid
Spain. (✕, ☺)

North South Agency
28 Wellington Road, Hastings, E. Sussex, TN34 3RN
U.K. (ᛁᛁ)
Tel. 01424 422364

Novotels
Calle Albacete 1, 28037 Madrid
Spain. (✕, ☺)

Santos Hotels
Calle Juan Bravo 8, Madrid
Spain. (✕, ☺)

SCI-SCCT Catalunya
Rambla Catalunya, 5 Pral 2na, 08007 Barcelona
Spain. (❤)

Sol Group
Calle Gremio Toneleros 42, 07009 Palma de Mallorca
Spain.
(✕☺)

The Au Pair Agency
231 Hale Lane, Edgware, Middlesex, HA8 9QF
U.K. (ᛁᛁ)
Tel. 0181 958 1750

Universal Care Ltd
Chester House, 9 Windsor End, Beaconsfield, HP9 2JJ
U.K. (🛗)
Tel. 01494 678811

Wimpey Club
Bena Vista, Malaga
Spain. (✖, 🌐)

Job Agencies

National Employment Service

Instituto Nacional de Empleo (INEM)
General Pardinas 5, Madrid
Spain.

Newspapers

El Pais
Diario 16
El Diario de la Costa del Sol
El Correo de Andalucia

English-language
Sur
Costa Blanca News
Iberian Daily Sun

Help with Travel and Accommodation

TIVE (Oficna Nacional de Intercambio y Tursimo
de Jovenes y Estudiantes)
José Ortega y Gasset 71, 28006 Madrid
Spain.

179

SWEDEN

Author's Comment. The country is sparsely populated but surprisingly sophisticated. Stockholm is a beautiful city-on-the-water and well worth a trip if you are touring Scandinavia.

Jobs You Can Do. Hotels often have casual work. There are also some jobs on farms and openings for au pairs.

What About Daily Life? Sweden is expensive. You will be hard-pressed to stay long if you do not have a job. Accommodation is costly and there are not many bargains in food and drink either.

Entry Regulations. EU citizens do not need a visa or a work permit. Other nationalities need a work visa which should be applied for after finding a job, but before leaving for Sweden.

Job Agencies

National Employment Service

Arbetsförmedlingen City
Box 634, Vasagatan 28-34
S101 30 Stockholm
Sweden.
Tel. 8 21 4300

Newspapers

Svenska Dagbladet
Dagen
Expressen
Dagnes Nyheter
Göteborg Posten

Job Leads

Eurocamp Plc
Knutsford, Cheshire WA16 0NL
U.K. (🏖)

IAL
Barangsgatan 23, 11641 Stockholm
Sweden. (❤)

International Farm Experience Programme
Stoneleigh Park, Kenilworth
Warwickshire, CV8 2LG
U.K. (☀)

North South Agency
28 Wellington Road, Hastings, E.Sussex, TN34 3RN
U.K.
Tel. 01424 422364 (👪)

Help with Travel and Accommodation

SFS Resebyra
Kungsgatan 4, P.O. Box 7144, 10387 Stockholm
Sweden.

SWITZERLAND

Author's Comment. Switzerland is a breathtaking country and any European trip should include at least a few days there. Geneva and Zurich are worth visiting and it is easy (if not especially cheap) to get around by train. If you are there in winter, do not miss the chance to work in a ski resort; it is the cheapest way to enjoy life in some of Europe's best spots and ski cheaply as well.

Jobs You Can Do. Most working travellers work in the tourist resorts, or spend a spell as an au pair.

What About Daily Life? Switzerland is a very expensive place to live so bring a sizeable emergency fund with you. Wages are high once you find a job. Many jobs in the tourist industry offer live-in accommodation, which is worth having.

Entry Regulations. Everyone wishing to work in Switzerland will need a combined work and residence permit. First, find a job with an employer who has been authorised to employ foreigners. Your employer will then apply for the permit. It can only be forwarded to you outside Switzerland. There is much unofficial work being done, but it is illegal.

Job Leads

Canvas Holidays
12 Abbey Park Place, Dunfermline, Fife, KY12 7PD
U.K. (🌐)

CFD
Falkenhoheweg 8, 3001 Bern
Switzerland. (♥)

Crystal Holidays
The Courtyard, Arlington Road, Surbiton, KT6 6BW
U.K. (🌐)
Tel. 0181 241 5111

Hotel Panorama Village
Villors sur Ollau
Switzerland. (✖, 🌀)

Internationale Arbeitsgemeinschaft
Rosengartenstrasse 17, 9000 St. Gallen
Switzerland. (❤)

Jobs in the Alps Agency
P.O. Box 388, London, SW1X 8LX
U.K. (✖, 🌀)

Kensington & Chelsea Nurses and Nannies
168 Sloane Street, London, SW1X 9QF
U.K. (👫)
Tel. 0171 581 5454

LZ
Postfach 728, Muhlegasse 13, 8025 Zurich
Switzerland. (⛲)

North South Agency
28 Wellington Road, Hastings, E.Sussex, TN34 3RN
U.K. (👫)
Tel. 01424 422364

Swiss Federation of Private Schools
Rue du Mont Blanc, Geneva 1
Switzerland. (✎)

SCI
Postfach 228, 3000 Bern 9
Switzerland. (❤)

Solihull Au Pair Agency
1565 Stratford Road, Hall Green, Birmingham, B28 9JA
U.K. (🛉)
Tel. 0121 733 6444

Village Camps
1296 Coppet
Switzerland. (🛉)

Willing Workers on Organic Farms
Speerstrasse 7, 8305
Dietikon
Switzerland. (🛉)

Newspapers

German-language
Neue Zurcher Zeitung
Basler Zeitung
Baslerstab
Berner
Zeitung
Berner Tagwacht

French-language
La Suisse
La Tribune de Genève (French-language)
Journal de Genève (French-language)

Help with Travel and Accommodation

Swiss Student Travel Office
SSR Reisen, Backerstrasse 4c, 8026 Zurich
Switzerland.

TURKEY

Author's Comment. Turkey is the country where East meets West and it offers a unique mingling of cultures which is hard to find anywhere else in the world. By Western standards, it is also incredibly cheap to stay there. Fun-lovers will head for the bustling tourist resorts on the southwest coast but a stay in Istanbul is a must.

Jobs You Can Do. The tourist industry offers casual work. There are opportunities for nannies and au pairs, and plenty of vacancies on voluntary work projects. You can try your hand teaching English in one of the many English-language schools in Istanbul and other cities.

What About Daily Life? Turkey is a Muslim country, no matter how close it is to the West, so respect the religious differences. Food, drink, accommodation and travel are still a bargain. Do not expect to be paid a lot, whatever work you do.

Entry Regulations. Everyone needs a working visa to work in Turkey. You can apply for it either before leaving or once you arrive in Turkey (your employer will do this for you). There is quite a lot of unofficial working, but it is illegal to enter as a tourist and then take up a job.

Job Leads

Benelux Resources Consulting Group
Cihangir Mah
Kargacisok 5, 34-840 Avcilar
Turkey.
(Various types of work.)

Gençtur
PO Box 1263, Sirkeci, Istanbul
Turkey. (♥)

GSM Youth Activities
Baylindir Sokak 45/7, Kizilay, Ankara
Turkey. (♥)

Jolaine Au Pair & Domestic Agency
18 Escot Way, Barnet, Herts, EN5 3AN
U.K. (👬)
Tel. 0181 449 1334

Silatur
11 Emek Ishani Kat, Kizilay, Ankara
Turkey. (♥)

Sunsail
Port House, Port Solent, Portsmouth, PO6 4TH
U.K. V (✖, 🌑, 👬, ⚠)
Tel. 01705 214330

Newspaper

Daily News (English-language newspaper)

Help with Travel and Accommodation

Gençtur
Yerebatan Caddesi 15/3, Sultanahmet, 34410 Istanbul
Turkey.

UNITED KINGDOM

Author's Comment. The U.K. offers a good range of working holiday opportunities, both for those already living there and others who are abroad. Most foreign visitors head for the London area, but jobs can also be found in other parts of the country where there is less competition from other travellers. If you have not visited the U.K. before, try to spend some time in London but also make time for travel to other places such as Scotland or Wales, which are culturally different from England.

Jobs You Can Do. Those that are especially popular with working travellers include farm work, fruit-picking, bar work, au pair work, nannying, conservation projects, work in tourist resorts and activity programmes for children.

What About Daily Life? The U.K. is cheaper than most of its European partners such as France and Germany, and you can find inexpensive food and accommodation in many places. It is much cheaper to travel by coach than by rail. Wages, especially for casual work, can be low.

Entry Regulations. EU citizens do not need a visa or a work permit. All other nationalities wishing to work should get a visa before leaving home, obtainable from the nearest British Consulate or High Commission. Citizens of other Commonwealth countries (including Canada, Australia and New Zealand) aged between 17 and 27 may take a working holiday in the U.K. for up to two years, for which they must obtain a permit from a British High Commission before leaving home. Those who have a grandparent born in the U.K. may stay for up to four years to look for work without the need to obtain a work permit. U.S. citizens who are full-time students can take on jobs in the U.K. on the Work in Britain Program.

187

Job Leads

In the U.K.

Academy Au Pair and Nanny Agency Ltd
42 Cedarhurst Lane
London, SE9 5LP. (⚥)
Tel. 0181 294 1191

Abbey Au Pairs
8 Boulnois Avenue, Parkstone, Poole
Dorset, BH14 9NX. (⚥)
Tel. 01202 732922

Albans Au Pair Agency
41 Station Road, Arlesley
Bedfordshire, SG15 6RG. (⚥)
Tel. 01462 731099

ATD Fourth World
48 Addington Street
London, SE5 7LB. (❤)
Tel. 0171 703 3231

Avalon Au Pairs
Thursely House, 53 Station Road, Shalford
Guildford, Surrey, GU4 8HA. (⚥)
Tel. 01483 63640

Bligh Appointments Ltd
131 Earls Court Road
London, SW5 9RH. (⚥, ⊞)
Tel. 0171 244 7277

Bourne Leisure Group Limited
51-55 Bridge Street, Hemel Hempstead
Herts, HP1 1LX. (⊛, ☒)
Tel. 01442 69257

British Trust for Conservation Volunteers (BTCV)
36 St. Mary's Street, Wallingford, Oxfordshire, OX10 0EU. (❤)
Tel. 01491 839766

Camp Beaumont
Bridge House, Orchard Lane
Huntingdon, PE18 6QT. (👬)
Tel. 01480 456123

CMP
186 St. Pauls Road, Balsall Heath
Birmingham, B12 8LZ. (❤)
Tel. 0121 446 5704

Concordia Youth Service Volunteers
8 Brunswick Place, Hove
Sussex, BN3 1ET. (⛷, ❤)
Tel. 01273 772086

Euroyouth Ltd
301 Westborough Road, Westcliff, Southend on Sea
Essex, SS0 9PT.
Tel. 01702 341434 (✎)

Helping Hands Au Pair & Domestic Agency
39 Rutland Avenue, Thorpe Bay
Essex, SS1 2XJ. (👪)
Tel. 01702 602067

189

International Voluntary Service
Old Hall, East Bergholt, Colchester
Essex, CO7 6TQ. (❤)

Jolaine Agency
18 Escot Way, Barnet, Herts, EN5 3AN. (👫)
Tel. 0181 449 1334

Just The Job
32 Dovedale Road, West Bridgford
Nottingham, NG2 6JA. (👫)
Tel. 0115 945 2482

Outback International
Pentney House, Narborough Road, Pentney
Norfolk PE32 1JD (🚣)

PGL
Alton Court, Penyard Lane, Ross On Wye
Herefordshire, HR9 5NR. (👫)
Tel. 01989 767833

Pontins Ltd
Saga House, The Green, Eccleston, Chorley
Lancs, PR7 5PH. (🌐)
Tel. 01257 452452

Scattergoods Agency
Thursley House, 53 Station Road, Shalford, Guildford
Surrey, GU4 8HA. ((❎, 🌐, 👫))
Tel. 01483 33732

TocH, 1 Forest Close, Wendover, Aylesbury
Buckinghamshire, HP22 6BT. (⚑, ❤)
Tel. 01296 623911

Towngate Personnel Ltd
65 Seamoor Road, Westbourne
Bournemouth, BH4 9AH.
(✖, in Channel Islands)

United Nations Association Wales
International Youth Service, Temple of Peace, Cathays Park
Cardiff, CF1 3AP. (❤)
Tel. 01222 223088

Universal Aunts
P.O. Box 304
London, SW4 0NN. (⚑, ⊞)
Tel. 0171 738 8937

Butlin's Holiday Worlds (U.K.)

Wonderwest World, Ayr
Scotland, KA7 4LB.
Tel. 01292 265141

Southcoast World
Bognor Regis
West Sussex, PO21 1JJ
Tel. 01243 822455

Somerwest World
Minehead
Somerset, TA24 5SH.
Tel. 01643 706333

Starcoast World
Pwllheli
Wales, LL53 6HX.
Tel. 01758 701441

Funcoast World
Skegness
Lincolnshire, PE25 1NJ.
Tel. 01754 762311
(T)

Outside the U.K.

SWAP Programme
P.O. Box 399, Carlton South, VIC3053
Australia.
(Programme entitling Australian students
to a Working Holiday Visa.)

Work in Britain Program
CIEE, 205 E 42nd Street, New York, NY10017
U.S.A.
(Programme entitling US students to a Working Holiday Visa.)
Tel. 212 661 1414

Job Agencies

Job Centres, run by the government's Employment Service, are located in most cities and towns.

Newspapers

Local newspapers in the area in which you wish to work have the best choice of vacancies. Also, many areas have a regional 'Jobs &

Careers' newspaper which contains only job advertising. In London, try the London Evening Standard.

Help with Travel and Accommodation

National Union of Students
461 Holloway Road, London, N7 6LJ
U.K.
Tel. 0171 272 8900

UKCOSA
60 Westbourne Grove, London, W2 5SH
U.K.
Tel. 0171 229 9268

Youth Hostels Association (England and Wales)
8 St. Stephen's Hill, St. Albans, Herts, AL1 2DY
U.K.
Tel. 01727 55215

UNITED STATES OF AMERICA

Author's Comment. The U.S.A. is a vast country and one of great contrasts—from the rugged peaks of the Rocky Mountains to sub-tropical Florida, and from the cities of New York and Los Angeles to the sleepy towns of the mid-west. Time in the U.S.A. is a must on any world trip. For a developed country, food, accommodation and travel are still remarkably cheap, so your budget will stretch far.

Jobs You Can Do. Although there is plenty of work on offer, the choice of legal work open to foreigners is very limited as work permits are difficult to obtain. Most foreign visitors working here do so as au pairs (there are plenty of jobs for women and men) or on voluntary work projects and exchange schemes. Many of these programmes allow you time to travel after work.

What About Daily Life? Food, accommodation and travel are reasonably priced and wages are attractive. Remember that distances are vast, so plan your travel carefully.

Entry Regulations. Check with your nearest American Consulate. Tourists from many countries require a visa although those from specified countries (including the U.K.) do not so long as they have a round-trip ticket. Anyone wishing to work must obtain a work visa before leaving for the U.S.A. These are readily granted for most au pairs and those on voluntary and exchange programmes, but almost impossible to obtain for other types of work.

Job Leads
British and Australian students should look into the BUNAC and SWAP schemes (addresses provided below) as these are two of the easier ways to secure a paid job.

Academy Au Pair & Nanny Agency Ltd
42 Cedarhurst Drive, London, SE9 5LP
U.K. (🛉)
Tel. 0181 294 1191

Au Pair in America
37 Queen's Gate, London, SW7 5HR
U.K. (🛉)

Avalon Au Pairs
Thursely House, 53 Station Road, Shalford
Guildford, Surrey, GU4 8HA
U.K. (🛉)
Tel. 01483 63640

Bingham Placements
9 Bingham Place, London, W1M 3FH
U.K. (👫)
Tel. 0171 224 4016

British Universities North America Club (BUNAC)
16 Bowling Green Lane, London, EC1R 0BD
U.K.
Tel. 0171 251 3472
(Various types of work for U.K. students only.)

Camp Counsellors
6 Richmond Hill, Richmond upon Thames TW10 6QX
U.K. (👫)

Camp Counsellors USA
420 Florence Street, Palo Alto, California, CA94301
U.S.A. (👫)

Campamerica
37a Queen's Gate, London, SW7 5HR
U.K. (👫)

Carnival Cruise Lines
5225 NW 87th Avenue, Miami, FL33718-2428
U.S.A.
(Opportunities on cruise ships.)

CIEE
205 East 42nd Street, New York, NY10017
U.S.A. (❤)

Council in International Education Exchange
33 Seymour Place, London, W1H 6AT
U.K.
Tel. 0171 706 3008
(For students only, enabling applicant to apply for any job.)

CTI Recruiting & Placement Agency Inc
1535 SE 17th Street, The Quay, Ft. Lauderdale FL33316
U.S.A.
(Opportunities on cruise ships.)

Disney Land
P.O. Box 10090, Lake Buena Vista, Florida, FL32830-0090
U.S.A. (⊚)
(For Working Holiday Visa holders only.)

Involvement Corps. Inc.
15515 Sunset Boulevard, Pacific Palisades, CA90272
U.S.A. (♥)

International Counsellor Exchange Program
38 W. 88th Street, New York, NY10024
U.S.A.
Tel. 212 787 7706 (👫)

Janet White Employment Agency
67 Jackson Avenue, Leeds, LS8 1NS
U.K. (👫)
Tel. 0113 266 6507

Norwegian Cruise Line
7665 Corporate Center Drive, Miami FL33126
U.S.A.
(Opportunities on cruise ships.)

Royal Caribbean Cruises
1050 Caribbean Way, Miami, FL33132-2601
U.S.A.
(Opportunities on cruise ships.)

SCI
Inisfree Village, Route 2, Box 506, Crozat, Virginia
U.S.A. (❤)

Student Conservation Association
P.O. Box 550, Charlestown NH03603
U.S.A. (❤)

SWAP
P.O. Box 399, Carlton South, Melbourne, VIC3053
Australia.
(Various types of work for Australian students only.)

USDA Forest Service
P.O. Box 18364, Washington DC20036
U.S.A. (❤)
Tel. 202 293 0922

Volunteers for Peace
Tiffany Road, Belmont, Vermont 05730
U.S.A. (❤)

Newspapers

Union Jack
P.O. Box 1823, La Mes. California, CA91944-823, U.S.A.
Tel. 619 466 3129
(For British/English-speaking expatriates and travellers in the
U.S.A.)

197

Help with Travel and Accommodation

Student Travel Network

Suite 307
Geary Street, San Francisco, CA94108
U.S.A.

and

Suite 728
6151 West Century Boulevard, Los Angeles, CA90034
U.S.A.

American Youth Hostels
1332 1 Street NW, Suite 800, Washington DC2005
U.S.A.

(Members are entitled to a wide range of discounts, starting at
10%, on travel, accommodation, food and entertainment.)

HOW TO APPLY TO ORGANISATIONS LISTED IN THIS CHAPTER

To find out what working holiday vacancies may be available at the present time, contact the employers and agencies listed in this chapter. Organisations listed in the Job Leads category are known to have regular vacancies that are suitable for working holidaymakers. However, the availability of these vacancies varies from time to time. At some times, there will be plenty of jobs available whereas at other times, there may be none. Also, note that requirements pertaining to age limit, experience, qualifications, nationality and so on are bound to vary. If an organisation you contact has no vacancies at the time you apply, try other organisations or reconsider your choice of destination.

When contacting the various organisations for further information, be sure to tell them:

- Your full name and address.
- The type of work you are interested in.
- The qualifications and skills you possess.
- When you are able to start work.
- How long you plan to stay.
- If you speak any foreign languages, as it will help your application.

When writing to addresses abroad, it is a good idea to enclose at least one International Reply Coupon (IRC) available from post offices in most countries. This will pay the postage on your reply letter. Be sure to allow plenty of time for a reply, especially when writing to a distant country or one where communication links are poor.

Chapter Six

WHERE TO FIND THAT EMBASSY

The following addresses are those of embassies in Australia, Canada, New Zealand, the U.K. and the U.S.A. The embassies can provide you with details of additional consulates in the respective countries, where these exist. When both countries involved are Commonwealth countries, remember that the embassy is known as a high commission.

AUSTRALIA

ALGERIA
13 Culgoa Circuit, O'Malley, Canberra, ACT 2600.
Tel. 062 861788

ARGENTINA
MLC Tower, Canberra, ACT 2606.
Tel. 062 824555

AUSTRIA
12 Talbot Street, Forrest, Canberra, ACT 2600.
Tel. 062 951533

BANGLADESH
11 Milneaux Place, Farrer, Canberra, ACT 2600.
Tel. 062 861200

BELGIUM
19 Arkana Street, Yarralumla, Canberra, ACT 2600.
Tel. 062 732502

BRAZIL
19 Forster Crescent, Yarralumla, Canberra, ACT 2600.
Tel. 062 732372

BRUNEI
16 Bulwarra Close, O'Malley, Canberra, ACT 2600.
Tel. 062 904801

CANADA
Commonwealth Avenue, Canberra, ACT 2600.
Tel. 062 733844

CHILE
10 Culgoa Circuit, O'Malley, Canberra, ACT 2600.
Tel. 062 864027

CHINA
15 Coronation Drive, Yarralumla, Canberra, ACT 2602.
Tel. 062 6273 4878

CYPRUS
37 Endeavour Street, Red Hill, Canberra, ACT 2600.
Tel. 062 953713

CZECH REPUBLIC
47 Culgoa Circuit, O'Malley, Canberra, ACT 2600.
Tel. 062 901516

DENMARK
15 Hunter Street, Yarralumla, Canberra, ACT 2600.
Tel. 062 732195-6

EGYPT
1 Darwin Avenue, Yarralumla, Canberra, ACT 2600.
Tel. 062 734437

FIJI
9 Beagle Street, Canberra, ACT 2600.
Tel. 062 959148

FINLAND
10 Darwin Avenue, Yarralumla, Canberra, ACT 2600.
Tel. 062 733800

FRANCE
6 Perth Avenue, Yarralumla, Canberra, ACT 2600.
Tel. 062 705111

GERMANY
119 Empire Circuit, Yarralumla, Canberra, ACT 2600.
Tel. 062 701911

GREECE
9 Turrana Street, Yarralumla, Canberra, ACT 2600.
Tel. 062 733011

HUNGARY
79 Hopetown Circuit, Yarralumla, Canberra, ACT 2600.
Tel. 062 823226-9

INDIA
3-5 Moonah Place, Yarralumla, Canberra, ACT 2600.
Tel. 062 733999

INDONESIA
8 Darwin Avenue, Yarralumla, Canberra, ACT 2600.
Tel. 062 733222

IRAN
14 Torres Street, Red Hill, Canberra, ACT 2600.
Tel. 062 952544

IRAQ
48 Culgoa Circuit, O'Malley, Canberra, ACT 2606.
Tel. 062 861333

IRELAND
20 Arkana Street, Yarralumla, Canberra, ACT 2606.
Tel. 062 733022

ISRAEL
6 Turrana Street, Yarralumla, Canberra, ACT 2600.
Tel. 062 731309

ITALY
12 Grey Street, Deakin, Canberra, ACT 2600.
Tel. 062 733333

JAPAN
112 Empire Circuit, Yarralumla, Canberra, ACT 2000.
Tel. 062 733244

KENYA
33 Ainslie Avenue, Canberra City.
Tel. 062 474688

KOREA (SOUTH)
113 Empire Circuit, Yarralumla, Canberra, ACT 2600.
Tel. 062 733044

MALAYSIA
7 Perth Avenue, Yarralumla, Canberra, ACT 2600.
Tel. 062 731543

MEXICO
14 Perth Avenue, Yarralumla, Canberra, ACT 2600.
Tel. 062 733905

NETHERLANDS
120 Empire Circuit, Yarralumla, Canberra, ACT 2600.
Tel. 062 733111

NEW ZEALAND
Commonwealth Avenue, Canberra, ACT 2600.
Tel. 062 733611

NIGERIA
7 Terrigal Crescent, O'Malley, Canberra, ACT 2600.
Tel. 062 861322

NORWAY
17 Hunter Street, Yarralumla, Canberra, ACT 2600.
Tel. 062 733444

PAKISTAN
59 Franklin Street, Forrest, Canberra, ACT 2603.
Tel. 062 950021-2

PAPUA NEW GUINEA
Forster Crescent, Yarralumla, Canberra, ACT 2600.
Tel. 062 733322

PERU
197 London Circuit, Canberra, ACT 2604.
Tel. 062 572953

PHILIPPINES
1 Moonah Place, Yarralumla, Canberra, ACT 2600.
Tel. 062 722535

POLAND
7 Turrana Street, Yarralumla, Canberra, ACT 2600.
Tel. 062 731211

PORTUGAL
23 Culgoa Circuit, O'Malley, Canberra, ACT 2600.
Tel. 062 901733

RUSSIA
78 Canberra Avenue, Griffith, Canberra, ACT 2603.
Tel. 062 959033

SAUDI ARABIA
12 Culgoa Circuit, O'Malley, Canberra, ACT 2600.
Tel. 062 862099

SINGAPORE
17 Forster Crescent, Yarralumla, Canberra, ACT 2600.
Tel. 062 733944

SOUTH AFRICA
State Circle, Yarralumla, Canberra, ACT 2600.
Tel. 062 732424

SPAIN
15 Arkana Street, Yarralumla, Canberra, ACT 2600.
Tel. 062 733555

SRI LANKA
35 Empire Circuit, Forrest, Canberra, ACT 2603.
Tel. 062 953521

SWEDEN
5 Turrana Street, Yarralumla, Canberra, ACT 2600.
Tel. 062 733033

SWITZERLAND
7 Melbourne Avenue, Forrest, Canberra, ACT 2603.
Tel. 062 733977

THAILAND
111 Empire Circuit, Yarralumla, Canberra, ACT 2600.
Tel. 062 731149

TURKEY
60 Mugga Way, Red Hill, Canberra.
Tel. 062 950227

U.K.
Commonwealth Avenue, Canberra, ACT 2600,
Tel. 062 706666

U.S.A.
State Circle, Yarralumla, Canberra, ACT 2603.
Tel. 062 705000

URUGUAY
Bonner House, Woden, Canberra.
Tel. 062 824418

VENEZUELA
MLC Tower, Woden, Canberra.
Tel. 062 824828

VIETNAM
6 Timbarra Crescent, O'Malley, Canberra, ACT 2600.
Tel. 062 866059

CANADA

ANTIGUA
60 St. Clair Avenue East, Toronto, M4T 1N5.
Tel. 416 961 3143

ARGENTINA
90 Sparks Street, Ottawa, K1P 5B4.
Tel. 613 236 2351-4

AUSTRALIA
50 O'Connor Street, Ottawa, K1P 6L2.
Tel. 613 236 0841

AUSTRIA
445 Wilbrod Street, Ottawa, K1N 6M7.
Tel. 613 563 1444

BANGLADESH
85 Range Road, Ottawa, K1N 8J6.
Tel. 613 236 0138-9

BARBADOS
151 Slater Street, Ottawa, K1P 5H3.
Tel. 613 236 9517-8

BELGIUM
85 Range Road, Ottawa, K1N 8J6.
Tel. 613 236 7267

BRAZIL
255 Albert Street, Ottawa, K1P 6A9.
Tel. 613 237 1090

BULGARIA
325 Stewart Street, Ottawa, K1N 6K5.
Tel. 613 232 3215

CHILE
151 Slater Street, Ottawa, K1P 5H3.
Tel. 613 246 9940

COLOMBIA
150 Kent Street, Ottawa, K1P 5P4.
Tel. 613 230 3760

COSTA RICA
150 Argyle Avenue, Ottawa, K2P 1B7.
Tel. 613 234 5762

CUBA
388 Main Street, Ottawa, K1S 1E3.
Tel. 613 563 0141

CZECH REPUBLIC
50 Rideau Terrace, Ottawa, K1M 2A1.
Tel. 613 749 4442

DENMARK
Range Road, Ottawa, K1N 8J6.
Tel. 613 234 0704

ECUADOR
150 Kent Street, Ottawa, K1P 5P4.
Tel. 613 238 2939

EGYPT
454 Laurier Avenue East, Ottawa, K1N 6R3.
Tel. 613 234 4931

FINLAND
55 Metcalfe Street, Ottawa, K1P 6L5.
Tel. 613 236 2389

FRANCE
42 Sussex Drive, Ottawa, K1M 2C9.
Tel. 613 232 1795

GERMANY
1 Waverley Street, Ottawa, K2P 0T8.
Tel. 613 232 1101

GREECE
76-80 MacLaren Street, Ottawa, K2P 0K6.
Tel. 613 238 6271

HONDURAS
151 Slater Street, Ottawa, HlP 5H3.
Tel. 613 233 8900

HUNGARY
7 Delaware Avenue, Ottawa, K2P 0Z2.
Tel. 613 232 1711

ICELAND
6100 Deacon Road, Montreal, H3S 2V6.
Tel. 514 342 6451

INDIA
10 Springfield Road, Ottawa, K2P 0L9.
Tel. 613 236 7403

INDONESIA
287 McLaren Street, Ottawa, K2P 0L9.
Tel. 613 236 7403

IRAN
411 Roosevelt Avenue, Ottawa, K2A 3X9.
Tel. 613 729 0902

IRAQ
215 McLeod Street, Ottawa, K2P 0Z8.
Tel. 613 236 9177

IRELAND
170 Metcalfe Street, Ottawa, K1P 6L2.
Tel. 613 233 6381

ISRAEL
50 O'Connor Street, Ottawa, K1P 6L2.
Tel. 613 237 6450

ITALY
275 Slater Street, Ottawa, K1P 5H9.
Tel. 613 232 2401

JAMAICA
275 Slater Street, Ottawa, K1P SH9.
Tel. 613 233 9311

JAPAN
255 Sussex Drive, Ottawa, K1N 9E6.
Tel. 613 236 8541

MALAYSIA
60 Bolteler Street, Ottawa, K1N 8Y7.
Tel. 613 237 5182

MEXICO
130 Albert Street, Ottawa, K1P 5G4.
Tel. 613 233 8988

MOROCCO
38 Range Road, Ottawa, K1N 8J4.
Tel. 613 236 7391

NETHERLANDS
275 Slater Street, Ottawa, K1P 5H9.
Tel. 613 237 5030

NEW ZEALAND
99 Bank Street, Ottawa, K1P 6G3.
Tel. 613 238 5991

NICARAGUA
170 Laurier Avenue West, Ottawa, K1P 5V5.
Tel. 613 234 9361

NIGERIA
295 Metcalfe Street, Ottawa, K2P 1R9.
Tel. 613 236 0521

NORWAY
90 Sparks Street, Ottawa, K1P 1R9.
Tel. 613 238 6571

PAKISTAN
151 Slater Street, Ottawa, K1P 5H3.
Tel. 613 238 7881

PERU
170 Laurier Avenue West, Ottawa, K1P 5V5.
Tel. 613 238 1777

PHILIPPINES
130 Albert Street, Ottawa, K1P SG4.
Tel. 613 233 1121

POLAND
443 Daly Avenue, Ottawa, K1N 6H3.
Tel. 613 236 0468

PORTUGAL
645 Island Park Drive, Ottawa, K1Y 0B8.
Tel. 613 729 0883

RUSSIA
285 Charlotte Street, Ottawa, K1N 8L5.
Tel. 613 235 4341

SAUDI ARABIA
99 Bank Street, Ottawa, K1P 6B9.
Tel. 613 237 4100

SOUTH AFRICA
15 Sussex Drive, Ottawa, K1M 6E2.
Tel. 613 744 0330

SPAIN
350 Sparks Street, Ottawa, K1R 7S8.
Tel. 613 237 2193

SWEDEN
441 MacLaren Street, Ottawa, K2P 2H3.
Tel. 613 236 8553

SWITZERLAND
5 Marlborough Avenue, Ottawa, K1N 8E6.
Tel. 613 235 1837

TANZANIA
50 Range Road, Ottawa, K1N 8J4.
Tel. 613 232 1509

THAILAND
180 Island Park Drive, Ottawa, K1Y 0A2.
Tel. 613 722 4444

TUNISIA
515 Oscannor Street, Ottawa, K1S 3P8.
Tel. 613 237 0330

TURKEY
197 Wurtemburg Street, Ottawa, K1N 8LN.
Tel. 613 232 1577

U.S.A.
100 Wellington Street, Ottawa, K1P 5T1.
Tel. 613 238 5335

URUGUAY
130 Albert Street, Ottawa, K1P 5G4.
Tel. 613 234 2727

NEW ZEALAND

ARGENTINA
142 Lambton Quay
Wellington.
Tel. 04 472 8330

AUSTRALIA
72 Hobson Street, Thorndon, Box 4036, Wellington.
Tel. 04 473 6411

AUSTRIA
22 Garrett Street, P.O. Box 6016, Wellington.
Tel. 04 801 9709

BELGIUM
1 Willeston Street, Box 3841, Wellington.
Tel. 04 472 9558

BRAZIL
135 Tamaki Drive, Mission Bay, Box 4356, Auckland.
Tel. 09 528 6681

CANADA
61 Molesworth Street, Box 12049, Wellington.
Tel. 04 473 9577

CHILE
1 Willeston Street, Box 3861, Wellington.
Tel. 04 472 5180

CHINA
2-6 Glenmore Street, Wellington.
Tel. 04 472 1382

COSTA RICA
50 Lunn Avenue, Mount Wellington, Box 686, Auckland.
Tel. 09 527 1523

CZECH REPUBLIC
12 Anne Street, Wadestown, Box 2843, Wellington.
Tel. 04 472 3142

FINLAND
25 Victoria Street, Box 1201, Wellington.
Tel. 04 472 4924

FRANCE
34-42 Manners St, Wellington.
Tel. 04 472 0200/201

GERMANY
90-92 Hobson Street, Thorndon, Box 1687, Wellington
Tel. 04 473 6063/4

GREECE
237 Willis Street, Box 27157, Wellington.
Tel. 04 484 7556

IRELAND
87 Queen Street, Box 279, Auckland.
Tel. 09 302 2867

INDIA
180 Molesworth Street, Box 4045, Wellington.
Tel. 04 473 6390/1

INDONESIA
70 Glen Road, Kelburn, Box 3543, Wellington.
Tel. 04 475 8697

215

ISRAEL
Plimmer City Centre, Box 2171, Wellington.
Tel. 04 472 2362

ITALY
34 Grant Road, Thorndon, P.O. Box 463, Wellington.
Tel. 04 473 5339

JAPAN
3-11 Hunter Street, Box 6340, Wellington.
Tel. 04 473 1540

MALAYSIA
10 Washington Avenue, Brooklyn, Box 9422, Wellington.
Tel. 04 485 2439

MEXICO
150-154 Willis Street, Box 3029, Wellington.
Tel. 04 485 2145

NETHERLANDS
Box 840, Wellington.
Tel. 04 473 9652

NORWAY
55 Molesworth Street, Wellington.
Tel. 04 471 2503

PAKISTAN
PO Box 3830, Auckland.
Tel. 09 528 3526

PAPUA NEW GUINEA
180 Molesworth Street, Box 197, Wellington.
Tel. 04 473 1560

PERU
199-209 Great North Road, Grey Lynn
Box 28083, Auckland.
Tel. 09 478 0366

PHILIPPINES
50 Hobson Street, Thorndon, Box 12042, Wellington.
Tel. 04 472 9848

POLAND
196 The Terrace, Box 10211, Wellington.
Tel. 04 471 2456

PORTUGAL
Southpac House, 1 Victoria Street, Wellington.
Tel. 04 472 1677

RUSSIA
57 Messines Road, Karori, Wellington.
Tel. 04 476 6113

SINGAPORE
17 Kabul Street, Khandallah, Box 29023, Wellington.
Tel. 04 479 2076

SPAIN
Box 71, Papakura, Auckland.
Tel. 09 5298 5176

SWEDEN
Greenock House, 39 The Terrace, Box 5350, Wellington.
Tel. 04 472 0909

SWITZERLAND
Panama House, 22 Panama Street, Wellington.
Tel. 04 472 1593

THAILAND
2 Cook Street, Karori, Box 17226, Wellington.
Tel. 04 476 8618

TURKEY
404 Khyber Pass Road, Newmarket, Auckland.
Tel. 09 522 2281

U.K.
Reserve Bank Building, 2 The Terrace
Box 1812, Wellington.
Tel. 04 472 6049

U.S.A.
29 Fitzherbert Terrace, Box 1190, Wellington.
Tel. 04 472 2068

UNITED KINGDOM

ALGERIA
54 Holland Park, London, WI1 3RS.
Tel. 0171 221 7800

ARGENTINA
53 Hans Place, London, SW1.
Tel. 0171 589 3104

AUSTRALIA
Australia House, The Strand, London, WC2B 4LA.
Tel. 0171 379 4334

AUSTRIA
18 Belgrave Mews West, London, SW1X 8HU.
Tel. 0171 235 3731

BARBADOS
1 Great Russell Street, London, WC1B 3NH.
Tel. 0171 631 4975

BELGIUM
103 Eaton Square, London, SW1W 9AB.
Tel. 0171 235 5422

BOLIVIA
106 Eaton Square, London, SW1W 9AD.
Tel. 0171 235 2257

BRAZIL
32 Green Street, London, W1Y 3FD.
Tel. 0171 499 0877

BULGARIA
186 Queen's Gate, London, SW7 3HL.
Tel. 0171 584 9400

CANADA
MacDonald House, 1 Grosvenor Square, London, W1X 0AB.
Tel. 0171 629 9492

CHILE
12 Devonshire Street, London, W1N 2DS.
Tel. 0171 580 6392

CHINA
49 Portland Place, London, W1N 3AH.
Tel. 0171 636 9375

COLOMBIA
3 Hans Crescent, London, SW1 0LR.
Tel. 0171 589 9177

CUBA
167 High Holborn, London, WC1 2AR.
Tel. 071 240 2488

CYPRUS
93 Park Street, London, W1Y 4ET.
Tel. 0171 499 8272

CZECH REPUBLIC
26-30 Kensington Palace Gardens, London, W8 4QX.
Tel. 0171 243 1115

DENMARK
55 Sloane Street, London, SW1X 9SR.
Tel. 0171 235 1255

DOMINICA
1 Collingham Gardens, London, SW5 0HW.
Tel. 0171 370 5194

DOMINICAN REPUBLIC
5 Braemar Mansions, Cornwall Gardens, London, SW7 4AG.
Tel. 0171 937 1921

ECUADOR
3 Hans Crescent, London, SW1X 0LS.
Tel. 0171 584 1367

EGYPT
26 South Street, London, W1Y 8EL.
Tel. 0171 499 2401

FINLAND
38 Chesham Place, London, SW1X 8HW.
Tel. 0171 235 9531

FRANCE
58 Knightsbridge, London, SW1X 7JT.
Tel. 0171 201 1000

GERMANY
23 Belgrave Square, London, SW1X 8PZ.
Tel. 0171 235 5033

GHANA
13 Belgrave Square, London, SW1X 8PR.
Tel. 0171 235 4142

GREECE
1A Holland Park, London, W11 3TP.
Tel. 0171 727 8040

HONDURAS
115 Gloucester Place, London, W1H 3PJ.
Tel. 0171 4880

HUNGARY
35 Eaton Place, London, SW1.
Tel. 0171 235 4048

ICELAND
1 Eaton Terrace, London, SW1W 8EY.
Tel. 0171 730 5131

INDIA
India House, Aldwych, London, WC2B 4NA.
Tel. 0171 836 8484

INDONESIA
38 Grosvenor Square, London, W1X 9AD.
Tel. 0171 499 7661

IRELAND
17 Grosvenor Place, London, SW1X 7HR.
Tel. 0171 235 2171

ISRAEL
2 Palace Green, London, W8 4QB.
Tel. 0171 937 8050

ITALY
14 Three Kings Yard, London, W1Y 2EH.
Tel. 0171 312 2200

JAMAICA
50 St. James's Street, London, SW1.
Tel. 0171 499 8600

JAPAN
46 Grosvenor Street, London, W1X 0BA.
Tel. 0171 493 6030

KENYA
45 Portland Place, London, W1N 4AS.
Tel. 0171 636 2371

KOREA (SOUTH)
4 Palace Gate, London, W8 SNF.
Tel. 0171 581 0247

LUXEMBOURG
27 Wilton Crescent, London, SW1X 8SD.
Tel. 0171 235 6961

MALAYSIA
45 Belgrave Square, London, SW1X 8QT.
Tel. 0171 235 8033

MALTA
16 Kensington Square, London, W8 5HH.
Tel. 0171 938 1712

MEXICO
8 Halkin Street, London, SW1 0AR.
Tel. 0171 235 6393

MOROCCO
49 Queen's Gate Gardens, London, SW7 5NE.
Tel. 0171 581 5001

NEPAL
12A Kensington Palace Gardens, London, W8 4QU.
Tel. 0171 229 1594

NETHERLANDS
38 Hyde Park Gate, London, SW7 SDP.
Tel. 0171 581 5040

NEW ZEALAND
New Zealand House, London, SW1Y 4TQ.
Tel. 0171 930 8422

NICARAGUA
8 Gloucester Road, London, SW7 4PP.
Tel. 0171 584 4365

NIGERIA
9 Northumberland Avenue, London, WC2 3EH.
Tel. 0171 839 1244

NORWAY
25 Belgrave Square, London, SW1X 8QD.
Tel. 0171 235 7151

PAKISTAN
35 Lowndes Square, London, SW1X 9JN.
Tel. 0171 235 2044

PARAGUAY
Braemar Lodge, Cornwall Gardens, London, SW7 4AQ.
Tel. 0171 937 1253

PERU
52 Sloane Street, London, SW1X 9SP.
Tel. 0171 235 1917

PHILIPPINES
199 Piccadilly, London, W1V 9LE.
Tel. 0171 493 3481

POLAND
47 Portland Place, London, W1N 3AG.
Tel. 0171 580 4324

PORTUGAL
62 Brompton Road, London, SW3 1BJ.
Tel. 0171 581 8722

ROMANIA
4 Palace Green, London, W8 4QD.
Tel. 0171 937 9666

RUSSIA
13 Kensington Palace Gardens, London, W8 4QX.
Tel. 0171 229 3628

SAUDI ARABIA
30 Belgrave Square, London, SW1X 8QB.
Tel. 0171 235 0831

SINGAPORE
2 Wilton Crescent, London, SW1X 8RW.
Tel. 0171 235 8315

SOUTH AFRICA
Trafalgar Square, London, WC2N SDP.
Tel. 0171 930 448

SPAIN
24 Belgrave Square, London, SW1X 8QA.
Tel. 0171 235 5555

SRI LANKA
13 Hyde Park Gardens, London, W2 2LU.
Tel. 0171 262 1841

SWEDEN
11 Montagu Place. London, W1H 2AL.
Tel. 0171 724 2101

SWITZERLAND
16-18 Montagu Place, London, W1H 2BQ.
Tel. 0171 723 0701

SYRIA
8 Belgrave Square, London, SW1X 8PH.
Tel. 0171 245 9012

THAILAND
29-30 Queen's Gate, London, SW7 SJB.
Tel. 0171 589 2944

TUNISIA
29 Prince's Gate, London, SW7 1QG.
Tel. 0171 584 8117

TURKEY
43 Belgrave Square, London, SW1X 8AP.
Tel. 0171 235 5252

UNITED ARAB EMIRATES
30 Prince's Gate, London, SW7 1RJ.
Tel. 0711 581 1281

U.S.A.
24-32 Grosvenor Square, London, W1A 1AE.
Tel. 0171 499 9000

URUGUAY
140 Brompton Road, London, SW1X 0DL.
Tel. 0171 584 8192

VENEZUELA
1 Cromwell Road, London, SW7 7RT.
Tel. 0171 584 4206

ZAIRE (DEM. REP. OF THE CONGO)
26 Chesham Place, London, SW1X 8HH.
Tel. 0171 235 6137

ZAMBIA
2 Palace Gate, London, W8 SNG.
Tel. 0171 589 6343

ZIMBABWE
429 Strand, London, WC2R 0SA.
Tel. 0171 836 7755

UNITED STATES OF AMERICA

ALGERIA
2118 Kalorama Rd NW, Washington DC 20008.
Tel. 202 265 2800

ARGENTINA
1600 New Hampshire Avenue NW, Washington DC 20009.
Tel. 202 939 6400

AUSTRALIA
1601 Massachusetts Avenue NW, Washington DC 20036-2273.
Tel. 202 797 3000

AUSTRIA
2343 Massachusetts Avenue NW, Washington DC 20008-2303.
Tel. 202 483 4474

BANGLADESH
2201 Wisconsin Avenue NW, Washington DC 20007.
Tel. 202 342 8372

BELGIUM
3330 Garfield Street NW, Washington DC 20008.
Tel. 202 333 6900

BOLIVIA
3014 Massachusetts Avenue NW, Washington DC 20008.
Tel. 202 483 4410

BRAZIL
3006 Massachusetts Avenue NW, Washington DC 20008-3699.
Tel. 202 745 2700

BULGARIA
621 22nd Street NW, Washington DC 20008.
Tel. 202 387 7969

CANADA
501 Pennsylvania Avenue, Washington DC 20001.
Tel. 202 682 1740

CHILE
1732 Massachusetts Avenue NW, Washington DC 20036.
Tel. 202 785 1746

CHINA
2300 Connecticut Avenue NW, Washington DC 20008.
Tel. 202 328 2500

COLOMBIA
2118 Leroy Place NW, Washington DC 20008-1895.
Tel. 202 387 8338

COSTA RICA
1825 Connecticut Avenue NW, Washington DC 20009.
Tel. 202 234 2945

CZECH REPUBLIC
3900 Linnean Avenue NW, Washington DC 20008-3897.
Tel. 202 363 6315

DENMARK
3200 Whitehaven Street NW, Washington DC 20008.
Tel. 202 234 4300

DOMINICAN REPUBLIC
1715 22nd Street NW, Washington DC 20008.
Tel. 202 332 6280

EGYPT
2300 Decatur Plaza NW, Washington DC 20008.
Tel. 202 232 5400

FINLAND
3216 New Mexico Avenue NW, Washington DC 20016.
Tel. 202 363 2430

FRANCE
4101 Reservoir Road NW, Washington DC 20007.
Tel. 202 944 6000

GERMANY
4645 Reservoir Road NW, Washington DC 20007-1918.
Tel. 202 298 4000

GHANA
3512 International Drive NW, Washington DC 20008.
Tel. 202 686 4500

GREECE
2221 Massachusetts Avenue NW, Washington DC 20008.
Tel. 202 939 5800

HONDURAS
3007 Tilden Street, Washington DC 20008.
Tel. 202 966 7702

HUNGARY
3910 Shoemaker Street NW, Washington DC 20008.
Tel. 202 362 6730

ICELAND
2022 Connecticut Avenue NW, Washington DC 20008-6194.
Tel. 202 265 6653

INDIA
2107 Massachusetts Avenue NW, Washington DC 20008-2811.
Tel. 202 939 7000

INDONESIA
2020 Massachusetts Avenue NW, Washington DC 20036.
Tel. 202 775 5200

IRELAND
2234 Massachusetts Avenue NW, Washington DC 20008.
Tel. 202 462 3939

ISRAEL
3514 International Drive NW, Washington DC 20008.
Tel. 202 364 5500

ITALY
1601 Fuller Street NW, Washington DC 20009.
Tel. 202 328 5500

JAMAICA
1850 K Street NW, Washington DC 20006.
Tel. 202 452 0660

JAPAN
2520 Massachusetts Avenue NW, Washington DC 20008.
Tel. 202 234 2266

KENYA
2249 R Street NW, Washington DC 20008.
Tel. 202 387 6101

KOREA (SOUTH)
2370 Massachusetts Avenue NW, Washington DC 20008.
Tel. 202 939 5600

LUXEMBOURG
220 Massachusetts Avenue NW, Washington DC 20008.
Tel. 202 265 4171

MALAYSIA
2401 Massachusetts Avenue NW, Washington DC 20008.
Tel. 202 328 2700

MEXICO
2829 16th Street NW, Washington DC 20009.
Tel. 202 234 6000

MOROCCO
1601 21st Street NW, Washington DC 20009.
Tel. 202 462 3611

NETHERLANDS
4200 Linnean Avenue NW, Washington DC 20008-1848.
Tel. 202 244 5300

NEW ZEALAND
37 Observatory Circle NW, Washington DC 20008-3686.
Tel. 202 328 4800

NICARAGUA
1627 New Hampshire Avenue NW, Washington DC 20008.
Tel. 202 387 4371

NIGERIA
2201 M Street NW, Washington DC 20037.
Tel. 202 822 1500

NORWAY
2720 34th Street NW, Washington DC 20008-2799.
Tel. 202 333 6000

PAKISTAN
2315 Massachusetts Avenue NW, Washington DC 20008.
Tel. 202 939 6200

PANAMA
2862 McGill Terrace NW, Washington DC 20008.
Tel. 202 483 1407

PARAGUAY
2400 Massachusetts Avenue NW, Washington DC 20008.
Tel. 202 483 6960

PERU
1700 Massachusetts Avenue NW, Washington DC 20036-1903.
Tel. 202 833 9860

PHILIPPINES
1617 Massachusetts Avenue NW, Washington DC 20036.
Tel. 202 483 1414

POLAND
2640 16th Street NW, Washington DC 20009.
Tel. 202 234 3800

PORTUGAL
2125 Kalorama Road NW, Washington DC 20008-1619.
Tel. 202 328 8610

ROMANIA
1607 23rd Street NW, Washington DC 20008.
Tel. 202 232 4747

RUSSIA
1125 16th Street NW, Washington DC 2008-4801.
Tel. 202 628 7551

SAUDI ARABIA
601 New Hampshire Avenue NW, Washington DC 20037.
Tel. 202 342 3800

SINGAPORE
1824 R Street NW, Washington DC 20009-1691.
Tel. 202 265 7915

SOUTH AFRICA
3051 Massachusetts Avenue NW, Washington DC 20008-3693.
Tel. 202 232 4400

SPAIN
270 15th Street NW, Washington DC 20009.
Tel. 202 265 0190

SWEDEN
600 New Hampshire Avenue NW, Washington DC 20037-2462.
Tel. 202 944 5600

SWITZERLAND
2900 Cathedral Avenue NW, Washington DC 20008-4405.
Tel. 202 745 7900

TANZANIA
2139 R Street NW, Washington DC 20008.
Tel. 202 939 6125

THAILAND
2300 Kalorama Road NW, Washington DC 20008.
Tel. 202 483 7200

TURKEY
1606 23rd Street NW, Washington DC 20008.
Tel. 202 387 3200

UGANDA
5909 16th Street NW, Washington DC 28006-2816.
Tel. 202 726 7100

U.K.
3100 Massachusetts Avenue NW, Washington DC 20008.
Tel. 202 462 1340

URUGUAY
1918 F Avenue NW, Washington DC 20006.
Tel. 202 331 1313

VENEZUELA
2445 Massachusetts Avenue NW, Washington DC20008.
Tel. 202 797 3800

ZAIRE (DEM. REP. OF THE CONGO)
1800 New Hampshire Avenue NW
Washington DC 20009-1697.
Tel. 202 234 7690

ZAMBIA
2419 Massachusetts Avenue NW
Washington DC 20008-2805.
Tel. 202 265 9717

NOTES

NOTES

INDEX